23: PERSPECTIVES IN CRITICISM

PERSPECTIVES IN CRITICISM

23:

ALBERT O. WLECKE

Wordsworth
and the Sublime

UNIVERSITY OF CALIFORNIA PRESS
Berkeley Los Angeles London
1973

Copyright © 1973 by The Regents of the University of California
University of California Press
Berkeley and Los Angeles, California
University of California Press, Ltd.
London, England

ISBN: 0-520-02233-5
LIBRARY OF CONGRESS CATALOG CARD NO.: 79-189218
Printed in the United States of America

For my mother

Preface

THIS STUDY does not offer a set of readings of Wordsworth's poems, and those who seek that should go elsewhere. Rather, it is the aim of this book to develop a description of Wordsworth's act of imagination. Throughout I have been influenced by a suspicion that William Blake once voiced in an annotation to his copy of the 1815 edition of Wordsworth's poems: "I do not know who wrote these Prefaces: they are very mischievous & direct contrary to Wordsworth's own Practise." My suspicion does not run so deep as Blake's; and I am often content to help along my analysis of Wordsworth's practice by taking a sentence or two, not only from the Prefaces, but from other passages in Wordsworth where he seems to be offering an *explanation*, as opposed to an *expression*, of the way in which imagination acts for him. But the trouble with Wordsworth's explanations of the ways of his consciousness, as Earl R. Wasserman has observed, is that they are inconsistent and varied; we can find Wordsworth offering "almost every variety of epistemological hypothesis" in his attempts to explain the business his imagination has with nature.* Wordsworth's very inconsistency as an explainer of his mental acts invites us to form our own, hopefully more consistent, hypotheses.

* Earl R. Wasserman, "The English Romantics: The Grounds of Knowledge," *Romanticism: Points of View*, ed. Robert F. Gleckner and Gerald E. Enscoe, 2d ed. (Englewood Cliffs, N. J., 1970), p. 337.

My special focus in this essay is upon the "visionary" imagination of Wordsworth. I concentrate upon those acts of Wordsworth's consciousness, so hauntingly expressed in his poetry, which seem to be making contact with realities more mysterious and provocative than those normally encountered in the universe of non-visionary perception. In my first chapter I advance a hypothesis about one of Wordsworth's most famous visionary acts—his "sense sublime" in "Tintern Abbey" of "something far more deeply interfused"—a hypothesis that seeks to explain, in a way Wordsworth's language clearly does not, the structure of consciousness involved in that moment of vision. In subsequent chapters I attempt to corroborate this hypothesis, to explore its full import, and to extend its relevance to other visionary acts described in Wordsworth's poetry. This approach thus moves me in the direction of presenting a generic description of the structure of Wordsworth's imaginative act, a description that stands, rather like a Platonic idea, above and apart from Wordsworth's always evolving practice, and is designed to suggest a single principle of intelligibility for as much of Wordsworth as possible.

There can be no doubt that there were changes in the way Wordsworth chose to use, as well as understand, his imagination during the most fruitful period of his creative activity, a period beginning about the time of the publication of the *Lyrical Ballads* (1798) and certainly not extending beyond the publication of *The Excursion* (1814). I am well aware that my approach precludes any possibility of giving an account of those changes, many of them significant. But since my whole analysis is pointed toward an increased understanding of one of the major goals of Wordsworth's poetic career, that proclaimed in the "Prospectus" of *The Excursion* of marrying his mind to nature, I am willing to surrender that possibility. The loss of the historical point of view is, I trust, partially compensated for by the kind of clarity I am thereby enabled to establish.

My approach also leads me away from the possibility of giving any detailed attention to the problem of Wordsworth's diction, especially to the question of how Wordsworth sometimes manages to arouse intimations of sublimity with words that "speak of nothing more than what we are," indeed with words that are often perilously close to justifying Coleridge's famous complaint about Wordsworth's matter-of-factness. This stylistic paradox, so disturbing to some of Wordsworth's first readers, is obviously related to the concerns of this essay. I hope that what I have to say about Wordsworth's act of imagination throws some indirect light. But I cannot engage the problem directly, for the kind of phenomenologically oriented vocabulary I employ does not seem easily to allow detailed stylistic consideration. Nor, for the sake of such consideration, do I wish so to extend and multiply the meanings of my key terms that any hope for an argument, both economical and clear, must be abandoned.

My intellectual debts are many, and I remember what I can in my notes. Since throughout I attempt to sustain a single argument as rigorously as possible, I also use these notes occasionally to introduce valuable perspectives that, if allowed into the main body of the text, might have obscured the focus of my argument. Furthermore, to sustain that focus, I take the liberty now and then of halting the flow of the argument—as, for example, in the middle of chapter 1—and of commenting upon its structure and rationale. I would rather risk the appearance of gratuitous delay than the appearance of gratuitous wandering.

Friends, teachers, and colleagues who have helped are, if not legion, at least too many to mention here. But I must remember James C. G. Conniff who first taught me to appreciate Wordsworth and to wonder about the mysteries of his deceptively simple language.

I must also thank colleagues in the English Department at the University of California, Irvine: Peter Clecak, Murray Krieger, Frank Lentricchia, and Ed Schell. They read the manuscript in whole or in part and made many valuable suggestions. Both Hazard Adams and Howard Babb, my chairmen at UCI during the writing of this book, influenced me as much by their example as by their kind and perceptive criticism. Lore Metzger, whose task was to supervise the original draft of this work, deserves special thanks for her valuable and unfailing encouragement and understanding. Bernard Paris, as he well knows, has helped me in ways he can never fully appreciate. The same must be said for Mary Butler. I also wish to thank Mrs. Suzanne Paulson for her expert typing and Mrs. Shirley Warren of the UC Press for her conscientious editorial assistance. Finally, a debt of friendship must be acknowledged to John Huddleston who always accepted the dubious task of reading every fresh page, and who never complained while pointing out so much that was imperfect.

A. O. W.

University of California, Irvine

Contents

To have a genius is to live in the universal, to know no self but that which is reflected not only from the faces of all around us, our fellow creatures, but reflected from the flowers, the trees, the beasts, yea from the very surface of the [waters and the] sands of the desert. A man of genius finds a reflex to himself, were it only in the mystery of being.

—Samuel Taylor Coleridge,
THE PHILOSOPHICAL LECTURES

1

The Argument

WHEN READERS of William Wordsworth speak of his "natural mysticism" or of his "pantheism," they almost invariably have in mind, as the principal support of these impressions, that famous passage from Wordsworth's meditation "Lines Composed a Few Miles above Tintern Abbey":

> And I have felt
> A presence that disturbs me with the joy
> Of elevated thoughts; a sense sublime
> Of something far more deeply interfused,
> Whose dwelling is the light of setting suns,
> And the round ocean and the living air,
> And the blue sky, and in the mind of man:
> A motion and a spirit, that impels
> All thinking things, all objects of all thoughts,
> And rolls through all things.[1]

That these lines are conducive to an impression on even a wary reader of "natural mysticism" is evident enough.[2] If by mysticism we simply understand an experience of direct contact with some kind of transcendent "spirit," then we have here Wordsworth's unmistakable testimony to his mysticism. There is also a suggestion in the first two lines of the passage that Wordsworth is susceptible to recurring transcendent encounters: the shift in tense from "have felt" to "disturbs" intimates a mental action rising out of the past and flowing into the present, almost as if Wordsworth, remembering his previous contacts with the "presence," is reexperiencing that "presence" and the accompanying "joy / Of elevated thoughts" in the very act of composing these lines.

That this mysticism is "natural"—and one way of taking "natural" is to understand "*not* supernatural"—can be seen if, first of all, we observe that Wordsworth's transcendent "something" is clearly not the supernatural and highly personal God of the Old and New Testaments, nor any other personal God of whatever tradition. Second, this blank but existent "something" is ubiquitous *within* nature; not a word is given of its having any existence "outside of," "beyond," or "above" nature, three usual prepositional ways of paraphrasing some sense out of the word "supernatural." Wordsworth's insistence that the "presence" is universally "interfused" and his catalog of its dwelling-places, albeit none of them especially confining, suggest that he wishes to keep the location of the ubiquitous "presence" thoroughly within the natural world, despite the flight of elevated thoughts. He makes no claim of having been rapt away to a seventh heaven or of having been Beatrice-led to a culminating vision of an unfolding celestial rose. In addition, this "sense sublime," as other passages in "Tintern Abbey" make quite clear, is one of the "gifts" (l. 86) nature herself provides to compensate Wordsworth for the sadness he experiences as he recognizes the encroachments of his mortality. And, without at this point questioning this theme of compensation, we might wonder how nature can bestow something unless it is hers to bestow. As the schoolmen used to phrase it: *nemo dat quod non habet.*

The use of this passage to support an assertion of Wordsworth's "pantheism" is far less tenable.[3] The four, insistently climactic "all's" of the last two lines, might suggest a Spinozistic vision of the Single Substance. But if we look more closely, we see that Wordsworth's language, even as it surges *toward* a statement of absolute cosmic oneness, is still capable of making kinds of distinctions inimical to a thoroughgoing pantheism. The interfused "something" may be an activity that is ubiquitous—"rolls through all things"—but its relationship to the specific objects of the universe Wordsworth names in this passage—"light of setting suns," "round ocean," "living air," "blue sky," "mind of man"—is one of neither identity nor that lesser degree of identity, consubstantiality. The relationship is rather one of dweller to dwelling-place. The metaphor whereby Wordsworth prevents his "something" from being located in a supernatural dimension also preserves distinctions within the natural. The dweller, we remind ourselves, is not the same thing as the dwelling-place. And a reader seeking to make Wordsworth appear vaguely orthodox (and certainly, therefore, not pantheistic) might claim that the relationship remotely resembles the old scholastic notion of God's immanence "within" creation as a Power continuously sustaining all things in being.[4] This notion prompted another nineteenth-century poet, Gerard Manley Hopkins, to some of his finest poems.[5] Or this same reader, focusing upon this transcendent something's activity within the mind of man, might be reminded of the Augustinian discipline of searching for an awareness of God within the depths of the soul.[6] But of course Wordsworth is neither a scholastic nor an Augustinian. Nor is he a doctrinaire pantheist. A meditation like "Tintern Abbey," wrestling as it does with the reality of human change and with the necessity of finding succor beneath the riddling weight of mortality, hardly can have as its doctrinal base the premise of the Single Substance. For from the perspective of such a premise real change is, in the last analysis, illusory. And such a premise, extrapolated from this single passage by a reader anxious for recognizable doctrine, would make the rest of this brooding poem irrelevant.

3

There is still another way in which the characterization of this passage as an expression of "natural mysticism" can be seen as superior to the characterization "pantheism." The latter term fails, not only because of the reasons given but also because of the approach its use implies. This approach takes an expression of a certain kind of experience as an expression of a commitment to a certain philosophical or, if you will, theological position. This kind of critical "taking" or *reductio ad doctrinam* tends to ignore that major characteristic of Wordsworth's best introspective verse: an almost Adamite empiricism before the rich ambiguities of experience, a desire to be so strictly honest in recording the full and often contradictory range of these experiences that no amount of position-naming or doctrinal labeling by the critic can provide an adequate account of the basis of his poetry, least of all these lines.[7]

For this reason an interpretation of these lines as an expression of a purported belief in an *anima mundi* also fails.[8] Whether Wordsworth entertained such a belief at times in his poetry, or whether indeed this belief is in some way involved here in his testimony of an encounter with a transcendent "presence," is a question that finally misses the point. Such a belief did not *produce* the experience for Wordsworth. Nor would, I imagine, the most passionate intellectual commitment to the notion of the existence of an *anima mundi* ever necessarily put anyone into direct, feeling contact with a ubiquitous "something." Such a notion might have provided Wordsworth with a conveniently traditional myth—certainly not explicit in "Tintern Abbey"—useful for expressive purposes. But expressive of what? The quality of his own experience of the world. We are reminded of his use of the myth of preexistence in the "Immortality Ode." Wordsworth explicitly tells us in the Fenwick note to the poem that he does not recommend the myth for our belief but uses it, as a poet is presumably entitled to, to provide a structure for his investigation into the mysteries of his changing perception of the world as he passes from youth to maturity.[9]

The moral, it seems to me, is this: for Wordsworth experience, mystical or otherwise, tends to precede doctrine. And therefore we best approach his testimony to a "presence" by taking it as the result, quite simply, of the fact that he has indeed "felt" this presence—and perhaps is feeling it again at the very moment of composition. We might, if we choose to, characterize this way of feeling as "natural mysticism." But we must remember that Wordsworth's testimony is not the result of obeisance to any intellectual position or commitment but emerges out of an empirical act, out of, as he tells us in lines 108 and 109 immediately following this passage, "nature and the language of the sense" which for him is the "anchor" of his "purest thoughts." And his awareness of "something far more deeply interfused" is a function of a "sense sublime." Surely if this awareness were related to, and perhaps determined by, a previously held and articulated doctrine, Wordsworth might have given us an epithet more informative than the groping "something."

II

My purpose in this essay is to investigate that structure of Wordsworth's experience that he refers to in "Tintern Abbey" as a "sense sublime." I take this "sense sublime" as a certain mode of consciousness or, to borrow a word from the phenomenologists, as an "intentionality." "Intentionality" has been described by Franz Brentano as an essential characteristic of any psychic phenomenon (as opposed to physical phenomenon). This characteristic is, quite simply, the fact that consciousness in any of its acts always exhibits "direction towards an object." [10] There is never merely consciousness but always consciousness *of*. Now the intended object of Wordsworth's "sense sublime" is, as he tells us, "something far more deeply interfused." To what extent, by investigating the nature of the intentionality characterized in the phrase "sense sublime," can we come to an understanding of that "direction" of Wordsworth's consciousness which puts him into contact with his transcendent "something"? To what extent, also, can such an investigation put us in a position to clarify and deepen our understanding of the poet's terribly empty yet terribly provocative term "something"?

The first thing to notice is that the poet's description of his intended object supplies us with clues as to the nature of his intentionality. The fact that his consciousness is directed for the moment toward nothing more explicit than a "something"—not toward a traditional and therefore nameable God, not toward the Single Substance of Spinoza, not toward the mythic *anima mundi*—suggests an intentionality that has moved beyond the possibility of discovering a precise name for its object. The poet, attempting to describe this act of consciousness, cannot specify it with reference to an explicit object. It is not that Wordsworth here is engaging in a cheap rhetorical gesture, seeking to provoke through the cultivation of inexplicability. Nor is it that Wordsworth himself feels any doubt about the reality of his intended object. Indeed, the fact that the poet chooses to express himself as encountering simply a "something," instead of refining this awareness of "something" into a specific x or y, intimates that his consciousness is caught up in the act of recognizing the sheer existence, the sheer "presence," of its intended object; so much so, perhaps, the poet finds it impossible to confine and control its activity of recognition through the imposition of a single characterizing name. Whatever the "something" is, it most especially *is*. And consciousness, at this groping moment in the meditation, principally intends that act of existence.[11]

Next we note that this "something" is "interfused," a word I take in its root sense, "to be poured between"

(L. *interfusus,* p.p. of *interfundere,* to pour between).[12] The something's activity of interfusion, as the rest of the passage makes clear, is ubiquitous throughout the cosmos. It is, like a universal ether, both poured out between all things and, since its "dwelling" is everywhere including the "mind of man," poured out *within* all things. The catalog of dwellings suggests an activity of consciousness in which the mind can find no solid purchase upon the visible cosmos. The dwellings of the interfused "something" are variously transparent ("living air," "blue sky") or suggestive of depths ("round ocean") or in the process of dissolving ("light of setting suns"). Even the "mind of man," the last mentioned dwelling-place, becomes, by virtue of its partnership in this list, suggestively transparent, dissolving, full of depths. The action of consciousness, therefore, which intends this universally interfused "something" is an action whereby the mind itself moves beyond a fixed attachment to a specific location, pours and spreads itself throughout the space of the visible cosmos (and finds expressive form for this action through a catalog of dwellings, the terms of which, first of all, do not really localize and, second, tend to become interchangeable). We might say then that one of the characteristics of the "sense sublime" is that its "direction" is paradoxically to wander, to move always beyond, to move toward an encompassing vision of the totality of things. The mind itself becomes universally interfused with the ubiquitous "something," almost as if the mind had totally identified with the "motion" and the "spirit" dwelling within itself as well as throughout the cosmos. Another, perhaps more precise, way of putting this is to say that that intentionality Wordsworth refers to as a "sense sublime" tends to become indistinguishable from its intended object: we note that almost at the conclusion of this passage the poet describes the "something" as that which "impels" (L. *impellere,* to drive on) "all objects of all thoughts," as if to suggest that

7

this "something" is one with the very activity whereby Wordsworth's consciousness exhibits "direction towards an object." It would not seem amiss, therefore, to surmise that the poet's "sense sublime" refers to a very special form of self-consciousness.

III

If it is indeed true that the phrase "sense sublime" refers to a structure of Wordsworth's consciousness in which the act of intention and the intended object grow indistinguishable, then cannot we say, shifting into a Coleridgean idiom, that a "sense sublime" indicates a fusion of "subject" and "object"? [13] And that the "sense sublime" refers to an activity of the esemplastic power of the imagination during which consciousness becomes reflexively aware of itself as an interfusing energy dwelling within the phenomena of nature? That this is the case is the general thesis of this essay, a thesis that I hope to show has relevance far beyond "Tintern Abbey." To supply a preliminary indication that Wordsworth himself was not unaware, in theory as well as in practice, of the relationship between imagination and self-consciousness, I point to a sentence from his "Preface to Poems (1815)" where the poet, in discussing the "dissolving" and "separating" functions of the imagination, observes that these "alterations" proceed from, and are "governed by, a *sublime* consciousness of the soul in her own mighty and almost divine powers." [14]

But to argue my thesis in detail, I obviously cannot depend upon a single sentence from Wordsworth's prose nor upon a limited reading of the phrase "sense sublime" as it appears within a context already selected out of a much larger context, the whole of "Tintern Abbey." Thus, without abandoning my initial understanding of the phrase and using the phrase as the still point of these turning speculations, I intend to proceed centrifugally around it and progressively exchange and

8

extend the contexts within which we might examine its import. Since William Empson has already delivered the news with regard to the word "sense" in Wordsworth and has concluded, with somewhat of a sad perplexity, that the word is used by the poet to refer to everything from the simplest act of sense perception to the most visionary of experiences,[15] I cast my emphasis upon the word "sublime," or, to be more precise, upon those structures of Wordsworth's consciousness which might be characterized as "sublime." I do not mean to confine myself to an elaborate gloss on a few lines from a single poem; that would be a purgatory blind indeed. Rather, I hope so to extend the question of what exactly is the place of the "sublime," sense or otherwise, in Wordsworth's work that this study will develop into an essay on Wordsworth's theory and practice of the imagination. If my thesis is correct, then this larger discussion should corroborate my reading of the phrase "sense sublime" as it appears in "Tintern Abbey." [16]

That poem will be the first larger context to be investigated; and in the next chapter the principal question explored will be: to what extent can we see reflected in "Tintern Abbey," examining its theme, its imagery, its meditative progressions, that activity of imaginative consciousness in which the object of the mind's "direction" tends to become indistinguishable from the very act of the mind's "direction"; and in which, therefore, the mind discovers itself in the position of reflecting upon its own agency, though perhaps without acknowledging that discovery? Insofar as we can trace echoes of such a tendency throughout the poem, we have then opened a perspective whereby to view, in a different and distinctly phenomenological light, the organic unity of the poem. But note that the principle of organic unity which this kind of approach postulates is a certain activity of consciousness reflected throughout the poem, an activity that, in my judgment, surfaces most explicitly in Wordsworth's encounter with the transcendent "something." Some of the theoretical implications of reading a poem in this fashion, I consider subsequently. At this point I am content to rest on an implication of Coleridge's provocative observation that the creation of a poem brings the full soul of man into activity.[17] Why not, therefore, explore a poem for traces of this activity, this imaginative consciousness, even when it is not, properly speaking, the overt subject of the poem?

In the next two chapters I turn to certain theories about the nature of the "sublime," and attempt to evolve a context in terms of which the general relationship between Wordsworth and the "sublime" might be examined.[18] It is well known that the sublime was one of the primary categories of eighteenth-century aesthetics and was deeply involved in the evolution of certain characteristics of that century's taste in natural scenery: its cultivated fondness for "awful prospects"—large mountains, angry oceans, apocalyptic storms, stupefying chasms, horrid rocks, and so sublimely on.[19] I first examine, in a highly selective way, a number of the period's speculations about the experience of the sublime (I exclude discussion of the "literary sublime"). Then I turn to Coleridge's speculations upon the subject and try to suggest their relevance to Wordsworth. My purpose throughout these two chapters will not be to write a history of the aesthetics of the sublime; that work has already been nobly accomplished by Professor Monk.[20] Nor am I concerned with the history of ideas, and certainly not with ferreting out "sources" of the Wordsworthian sensibility, always a dubious pursuit with so original a poet. Instead, by sifting some of these theories, I hope to come up with notes toward what I call a "phenomenology of the sublime." I assume, along with Burke and Kant, that the sublime is a distinguishable category of conscious experience; to try and evolve my own descriptive generalities about the nature of this special experience will be useful in advancing my thesis.

I am not in these chapters writing an essay in formal aesthetics. Rather, the generalities or the "phenomenological notes" should be taken as nothing more than the results, occasionally idiosyncratic, of an attempt to provide for myself more sophisticated perspectives upon the import of my thesis. In other words, my assumption that the sublime is a distinguishable category of conscious experience is a useful fiction I employ to mediate between the implications of certain historically given theories of the sublime and my own exploration of Wordsworth, for the enrichment, I trust, of the latter.

In my final chapter I concentrate exclusively upon Wordsworth and briefly indicate how some of the phenomenological perspectives developed in the preceding chapters might be useful in evolving solutions to certain problems faced by any reader of the poet. The experience of the sublime, as will be abundantly clear at this point in the essay, is frequently involved with a certain experience of space. And since my thesis is concerned with a moment in Wordsworth's poetry when he feels an identification between his mind and a spatially extended "something," it seems a related task to attempt a general description of the traffic between the poet's imagination and the images of space his eye encounters. While much of this description will have been adumbrated in the preceding chapters, it will be useful, especially in a concluding chapter, explicitly to present a summary sketch of the nature of Wordsworthian space. But where there is a discussion of space, can a discussion of time be far behind? Thus in this chapter I also examine Wordsworth's very special sense of time, involved as it is with an act of memory so crucial to many of his best poems.

Finally, I examine what Meyer Abrams calls the "central paradox in the oracular passages of Wordsworth's major period: the oxymoron of the humble-grand, the lofty-mean, the trivial-sublime." [21] If the "sense sublime" of "Tintern Abbey" is for Wordsworth

11

his deepest intuition of the enduring nature of things, then perhaps he has the right to assume the potential sublimity of everything, even of the most trivial phenomena. For the universally in-dwelling "something," like Hopkins's "grandeur of God," can shine out of the "meanest flower that blows" as well as out of more likely places such as the sublime vistas of ocean and sky. But I believe that the paradox of *humilitas-sublimitas* can be taken as descriptive, not only of Wordsworth's deepest sense of the nature of the real but also of his explicitly formulated poetic program. And if my thesis is correct—namely, that the poet's "sense sublime" of a universally in-dwelling "something" is indeed a function of consciousness becoming reflexively aware of its own interfusing energies—we can also say that in the last analysis the "central paradox" of Wordsworth's major period is an expression of a recurring structure of his imaginative consciousness. This structure of consciousness is like that belonging to the Pedlar of "The Ruined Cottage," who "in the mountains did *feel* his faith" and directly saw that

> All things there
> Looked immortality, revolving life,
> And greatness still revolving, infinite;
> There littleness was not, *the least of things*
> *Seemed infinite.*[22]

Such a power of consciousness—to make the least seem infinite, the humble seem sublime—I take as perhaps the characteristic expression of Wordsworth's imagination. It is also a power closely related to a "sense sublime" capable of transcendent encounters.

IV

Throughout this essay there is a certain emphasis in how I choose to look at Wordsworth's poetry, an emphasis that now needs some explanation and justification. This emphasis emerges from a tendency, implicit in any expressive theory of art, to look upon the poem as an "exfoliation"—the organic metaphor is based on Coleridge's precedent [23]—of a certain state of the poet's consciousness. Such a way of reading tends to overlook the poem as, for example, a "well wrought urn," a structure in language possessing its own immanent verbal laws. It instead seeks to discover a way of characterizing the movement of the poet's mind as it engages with its materials and as this movement is embodied in the language of the poem. Thus, from this point of view, the proper subject of "The Solitary Reaper" is not the solitary, singing lass but the evolving drama of Wordsworth's conscious reactions to his memory of the girl. And thus the proper study of this changing reaction begins, and sometimes ends, with an effort to describe this *actio mentis*. In other words, my emphasis in this study might be called "phenomenological": I am concerned with *describing* certain structures of Wordsworth's consciousness as these are exhibited or implied in his poetry.

In his essay "Upon Epitaphs (3)" Wordsworth observes that words are to be ideally "an incarnation of the thought." [24] This metaphor rejects the curious distinction between word and thought implied in the popular eighteenth-century metaphor of words being the "clothing" of thought.[25] The metaphor also intimates, I believe, that a sequence of words in a poem by Wordsworth can be taken as an enactment of a certain sequence of thought or, better, of thinking. The word is not an overt statement of an already conceived thought, somehow separable from that thought as clothing is from a body. Rather, the relationship between word and thought is analogous to the relationship between body and soul: words "body forth" an otherwise hidden activity of the mind, they are one with that activity, and their progression is expressive of a certain progres-

13

sion in consciousness. I say "activity of the mind" and "progression in consciousness" because I wish to avoid the suggestion that the thought, or thinking, is exclusively or even necessarily discursive.[26] As Wordsworth tells us in the same essay, the "excellence of writing . . . consists in a conjunction of Reason and Passion," [27] and it is presumably this conjunction that finds embodiment in language. The metaphor of incarnation also seems to reject the highly rhetorical, audience-directed implications of the metaphor of clothing, implications perhaps most clearly seen in the *locus classicus* of this metaphor in eighteenth-century poetry, namely, Pope's observation that "True Wit is Nature to advantage dress'd, / What oft was thought, but ne'er so well express'd." [28] The metaphor of incarnation, however, has poet-directed implications: it invites us to question what "conjunction" of a poet's "Reason and Passion" has found its embodiment, its visible form, in the language of his poem.

My point is not to defend Wordsworth's position on the always perplexing question of the relationship between thought and language. The organicism of his position is evident—certainly his metaphor indicates an organic relationship—and perhaps can best be examined within the context of a study of the Romantic period's general commitment to the use of organic metaphors in analyses of the poetic process. I seek merely to suggest the grounds of my assumption that one of the productive ways of reading certain poems by Wordsworth is to take them as documents descriptive, explicitly and sometimes implicitly, of evolving structures of consciousness. What is *The Prelude* if not, among other things, just such an explicit document? [29] I make no theoretical defense of this approach—the subject is far too elaborate for the scope of this essay —but recall, first, Geoffrey Hartman's exemplary success in treating the poems in this wise, his describing single dramas of Wordsworth's mind in individual poems

as well as developing a history of the poet's consciousness through a series of poems.[30] Second, I think of
Wordsworth's own practice in explaining his sonnet
"With Ships the Sea Was Sprinkled Far and Nigh." In
a letter to Lady Beaumont he provides a reading that in
fact regards the poem as essentially a description of a
progression of conscious states. His commentary deserves to be quoted at length:

> I am represented in the sonnet as casting my eyes
> over the sea, sprinkled with a multitude of ships,
> like the heavens with stars. My mind may be sup-
> posed to float up and down among them, in a kind
> of dreamy indifference with respect either to this
> or that one, only in a pleasurable state of feeling
> with respect to the whole prospect. "Joyously it
> showed." This continued till that feeling may be
> supposed to have passed away, and a kind of com-
> parative listlessness or apathy to have succeeded,
> as at this line,
>
> Some veering up and down, one knew not why.
>
> All at once, while I am in this state, comes forth
> an object, an individual; and my mind, sleepy and
> unfixed, is awakened and fastened in a moment.
>
> Hesperus, that *led*
> The starry host
>
> is a poetical object, because the glory of his own
> nature gives him the pre-eminence the moment he
> appears. He calls forth the poetic faculty, receiv-
> ing its exertions as a tribute. But this ship in the
> sonnet may, in a manner still more appropriate, be
> said to come upon a mission of the poetic spirit,
> because, in its own appearance and attributes, it
> is barely sufficiently distinguished to rouse the cre-

15

ative faculty of the human mind, to exertions at all times welcome, but doubly so when they come upon us when in a state of remissness. The mind being once fixed and roused, all the rest comes from itself; it is merely a lordly ship, nothing more:

> This ship was nought to me, nor I to her,
> Yet I pursued her with a lover's look.

My mind wantons with grateful joy in the exercise of its own powers, and, loving its own creation,

> This ship to all the rest I did prefer,

making her a sovereign or a regent, and thus giving body and life to all the rest; mingling up this idea with fondness and praise—

> where she comes the winds must stir;

and concluding the whole with,

> On went she, and due north her journey took;

thus taking up again the reader with whom I began, letting him know how long I must have watched this favourite vessel, and inviting him to rest his mind as mine is resting.[31]

We can note in this "interpretation" how Wordsworth invites his reader to make a number of suppositions, all of them about the action of his mind, and none immediately explicit in the text of the poem. The first supposition we are to make is that the poet's mind is floating "up and down" among the ships in almost a Keatsian state of empathy. The poet's mind is "in a kind of dreamy indifference with respect either to this [ship] or that one, only in a pleasurable state of feel-

16

ing with respect to the whole prospect." This supposition is to be based upon the first quatrain of the sonnet:

> With Ships the sea was sprinkled far and nigh,
> Like stars in heaven, and joyously it showed;
> Some lying fast at anchor in the road,
> Some veering up and down, one knew not why.[32]

Only two statements in the quatrain seem to allow for any immediate inference about the state of mind of the observer: "joyously it showed" and "one knew not why." The impersonal phrasing of these two statements hardly indicates the strong presence of an individual onlooker. Yet Wordsworth asks his reader to suppose that the words of the quatrain, in addition to their descriptive function, suggest, through the objects named in the description, an activity of the poet's own consciousness. These words, then, have a double function; they point simultaneously in the directions of the observer and of the observed. For in naming the ingredients of the scene, they also presumably express (or embody) a certain activity of the mind, an activity that does not include—precisely because the mind is floating with "dreamy indifference"—a strong sense of personal identity. Hence, we might also infer, the impersonal phrasing of "joyously it showed" and "one knew not why."

The second supposition Wordsworth invites his reader to make would have us take this quatrain as an indirect description, not simply of a fixed state of consciousness but also of a progression in consciousness. In the fourth line we are to surmise Wordsworth's opening "pleasurable state of feeling" to "have passed away, and a kind of comparative listlessness or apathy to have succeeded." Whether we are to surmise this apathy from the image of the ships "veering up and down" or from the vaguely perplexed and emotionally flat tone of "one knew not why," is a difficult question to decide. Perhaps from both.

Wordsworth sees the next quatrain as illustrative of the willful exercise of the creative imagination:

A goodly Vessel did I then espy
Come like a giant from a haven broad;
And lustily along the bay she strode,
Her tackling rich, and of apparel high.

Wordsworth's commentary would have us understand that this ship, its appearance amplified through the elaborate and sustained simile of the striding giant, was in fact "barely sufficiently distinguished to rouse the creative faculty of the human mind." Strangely, however, it is precisely for this reason that the ship may be said to have "come upon a mission of the poetic spirit." The highly figurative vision of the second quatrain is to be taken as the result of the sudden intrusion of a ship "barely sufficiently distinguished" upon the point of view of an observer who is "in a state of remissness," "sleepy and unfixed." The abrupt fixation of Wordsworth's eye upon the single ship awakens the "I" of the poem—the personal point of view is mentioned for the first time in line 5—and triggers a release of the imagination, an exercise of creative power "doubly" welcome to the poet because of the immediately preceding state of "apathy" and "listlessness." (We might also note the oblique suggestion of reflexive imaginative consciousness in Wordsworth's observation that his stated preference for this "ship to all the rest" in line 11 is the result of the fact that his "mind wantons with grateful joy in the exercise of its own powers." The value of the ship is a function of the poet's recognition in the ship's imaginatively transfigured appearance of his own creative mind.) Thus, behind the overt statements of the first eight lines of this sonnet, Wordsworth asks his reader to envisage a progressive activity of consciousness in which the mind passes from a state of pleasurable passivity to a state of near torpor to a state of

18

meditation describes, reflections of that act of vision
ng which Wordsworth encounters an interfusing
nic presence; an encounter that dissolves distinc-
s between the activity of consciousness and the ac-
y of its intended object; an encounter that finally,
ve argued, is a manifestation of imaginative con-
usness becoming reflexively aware of its own ubiq-
us energies? This thesis, it must now be admitted,
ests that Wordsworth, even at that moment when
hetoric indicates a mind at the highest pitch of in-
ve certitude, is still struggling unawares with a
lexity: a consciousness of transcendence without
proper name for what is indeed the transcendent
t—his own mind. The tentative quality of Words-
h's vision and hope in "Tintern Abbey" is thus not
ly the result of the privacy of that vision and hope,
lack of sanction in terms of a traditional ortho-
Within the poet's very privacy there is a failure of
nition. He displaces his "sense sublime" of the
r of his own imaginative consciousness into a
thing" dwelling throughout the universe. And this
cement is but the most extreme of a series of dis-
ments of the recognition of imaginative activity
pervades the entire meditation.
clarify and support these generalities, I consider
em from two points of view: (1) as a poem about
ors; (2) as a meditation that proceeds as a con-
g exploration of the sense of interiors. The first
of view will bring us up against Wordsworth's
tent characterization of imaginative activity as a
on of a sense of immanence, of a "within," in
menal nature, and also up against the question of
deed this activity proceeds from a "depth" of the
far below the surface of ordinary consciousness.
econd point of view will enable us to see the
ative progressions of the poem as controlled, in
t least, by an explorative movement of the poet's
from one "interior" of consciousness to the next:

exultant creativity. The words of these lines, in addition
to their obvious descriptive functions, finally are sup-
posed to tell a tale of the poet's mind, a tale that, without the commentary of the poet himself, would certainly
not be immediately apparent.

Wordsworth's invitation in his letter to Lady Beaumont to suppose in this fashion is the final justification
I offer of that way of reading his poetry which I emphasize in this study. And with this invitation in mind, we
can turn to his "Lines Composed a Few Miles above
Tintern Abbey."

2

A Poem About Interiors

I

"Tintern Abbey" resembles the classical religious meditation in that it begins with a careful description of a
scene, with what Saint Ignatius would have called "the
composition of place." It also shows Wordsworth employing those three powers of the mind designated by
the ultimately Augustinian psychology from which the
religious meditation was derived: memory, understanding, and will. In the poem we find Wordsworth struggling to understand what his memory so poignantly reveals: his perception of nature has irrevocably changed
with the passing of years. We also find him making certain promises: he shall continue to turn to nature as
the "guide, the guardian of my heart, and soul / Of
all my moral being" (ll. 110–111). But despite these
similarities with the religious meditation, the atmosphere of Wordsworth's poem is vastly different. The
scene that is "composed" is significant only because of
the private resonances Wordsworth discovers in it. It
carries in its texture none of the traditional dimensions
of meaning that scenes from scripture had for the dis-
ciple of Saint Ignatius. Moreover, as Louis Martz has
pointed out, the kind of understanding "applied" is associative rather than, as in a meditation by Donne, dialectic.[1] And the moment of illumination toward which
this ruminating understanding gropes lacks the benefit
of an orthodox theology by which to guide itself. Finally, the resolution Wordsworth makes, his pledge of

20

continuing fealty to nature, is based
his past experience. His wish derives
or point from any traditionally sancti
tive.

Perhaps it is this complete absence
other than the private which makes
sion of Wordsworth's poem so diffe
pression left by a classical religious m
for example, find Donne struggling
with grave doubts about his own po
tion, but the fundamental coordina
are secure. And his precisely defin
often than not provides the alembic
are resolved. In "Tintern Abbey,"
worth's universe and his resolution
tive. The essential elements of his
questioned a number of times in
wish to find continuing sustenan
that grows out of his tentative vis
certainty of fulfillment that Do
Christian promises. In the conclud
Wordsworth even finds it necessa
Dorothy into the uncertain futur
sustain the necessary relationshi
even if he no longer can do so. B
nature and the version of "salvat
are so shot through with ambig
agree with what one critic has s
the "dominating mood of the g
worth's meditation along the ba
of perplexity."[2] This perplexit
what appears to be the most af
poem: Wordsworth can find
principle of cosmic oneness
"something."

We can examine the source
plexity by posing the followin
tent can we see, in the whole

a journey through a variety of mental depths. These two approaches will not permit us to unravel every strand of meaning in the poem, nor answer every question, and what follows is not to be regarded as an effort toward total explication (I exclude, for example, any consideration of the last verse paragraph). But they will at least serve to describe, in a way corroborative of my thesis, the grounds of Wordsworth's haunting perplexity.

II

"Tintern Abbey" is a poem preoccupied with the insides of things, with a sense of immanent power lurking beneath the surface of phenomena.[3] The "something," of course, is "deeply interfused" and dwells within all things. But even in Wordsworth's opening "composition of place" (ll. 1–22), the poet's eye and ear encounter a landscape permeated with immanence. The mountain springs of the Wye are heard as rolling with a "soft inland murmur," the word "inland" not only supplying a reason for the softness of the murmur but also obliquely evoking a much more extensive region than that seen in the poem, a region *within which* the immediate landscape around Tintern Abbey is located. The "wild secluded scene" of this landscape is seen by the poet as somehow impressed by "steep and lofty cliffs" with "Thoughts of a more deep seclusion," as if the elements of the scene were in themselves enacting the poet's sense of intensifying solitude. Wordsworth finds himself located in a kind of interior: "I again repose / Here, under this dark sycamore." He observes "orchard-tufts" which because of their "one green hue" seem almost to be submerging as they "lose themselves / 'Mid groves and copses." The "pastoral farms" of the scene barely emerge from the lush, enclosing landscape: they are "Green to the very door." The poet, noticing suggestive "wreaths of smoke" drifting up from among the trees

23

with "some uncertain notice," begins to shape hypotheses about the immanence of the woods. Perhaps the uncertain notice is of "vagrant dwellers in the houseless
woods." The quiet oxymoron "vagrant dwellers" prefigures the curious way in which Wordsworth will later
attempt to fix the location of the "something": its
"dwelling" turns out to be everywhere. Here, at the
opening of the meditation, the "dwellers" of the woods,
perhaps gypsies, are in fact wandering (L. *vagari*, to
wander); and it seems only fitting that they be located
where there are no fixed human locations. Their potential ubiquity within the "houseless" woods resembles
the ubiquity of the "something" within its universal
dwelling-places.

Finally Wordsworth surmises a "Hermit" sitting alone
at the quiet heart of the landscape. This surmise com-
pletes the centripetal movement of the poem's first verse
paragraph. The Hermit's presence is envisaged as not
only within the landscape (itself surrounded by a
larger, unseen region) but also within an enclosure itself contained by the woods—a "Hermit's cave." This
last interpretation by Wordsworth of the "uncertain
notice" is also the last refinement of his "Thoughts of
more deep seclusion." The "wild secluded scene," at the
moment when Wordsworth is about to turn away from
a direct contemplation of it, is thus sensed as possessing
an immanence—and is perhaps not so wild after all.
For the solitude enclosed within the landscape is surmised as a human solitude.

We might also characterize the progression of Wordsworth's mind in his initial meditative act as a movement
downward and inward: from the sight of "steep and
lofty cliffs" to a sense, beyond the reach of sight, of an
immanent human presence deep in the woods. And if
we try to characterize this progression in terms of a
larger context of metaphorical implication, we find useful Northrop Frye's observation that the "metaphorical
structure of Romantic poetry tends to move inside and

downward instead of outside and upward, hence the creative world is deep within, and so is heaven or the place of the presence of God." [4] Thus, we are tempted to ask of Wordsworth's composition of place whether it in fact is symbolic of a movement of his mind toward the sources of his creativity, whether the poet's preoccupation with the immanence of phenomena is not really a preoccupation with the creative power immanent within his own mind, and whether, finally, the movement downward and inward does not prefigure the poet's later encounter with his transcendent "something." To investigate these questions, we must step momentarily away from "Tintern Abbey" and consider at large Wordsworth's metaphorical geography of introspection.

I say "geography" because Wordsworth consistently tends to speak of his mind in metaphors implying spatial extent; thus the acts of introspection, of memory, of consciousness in general, all of which take place *within* this spatialized mind, can be likened to a movement within a special kind of spatial dimension or even to a journey through a certain region. What, then, are the main (physical and psychological) features of Wordsworth's interior landscape? We might say, first of all, that since Frye's observation suggests a metaphorical equation between the place where imaginative power is to be found and the place where—to borrow a term from Rudolf Otto—the "Holy" is to be encountered,[5] the journey into what has been referred to in Wordsworth as the "abysses of the subjective consciousness" is simultaneously a journey toward the numinous, the transcendent, even the awful.[6] And in terms of this geography of introspection, Wordsworth at times approaches his power of imagination with something of the same mixture of dread and desire that a soul of an earlier tradition might have experienced in feeling himself translated to the otherworld.

In the fragment of *The Recluse* which Wordsworth

includes in the preface to the 1814 edition of *The Excursion,* the poet deliberately recalls the Christian tradition of vision, only to express, with a certain bravado, his emotional indifference to it:

> Jehovah—with his thunder, and the choir
> Of shouting Angels, and the empyreal thrones—
> I pass them unalarmed.

Instead, Wordsworth discovers his terror of the "Holy" in the journey "inside and downward"—in the visionary act of introspection. In lines immediately following his almost contemptuous dismissal of Jehovah's "shouting Angels," he writes:

> Not Chaos, not
> The darkest pit of lowest Erebus,
> Nor aught of blinder vacancy, scooped out
> By help of dreams—can breed such fear and awe
> As fall upon us often when we look
> Into our Minds, into the Mind of Man—
> My haunt, and the main region of my song.[7]

Wordsworth's otherworld is thus an underworld, not that created by Miltonic vision but that discovered by consciousness turning inward upon itself. The negative comparisons of these lines curiously suggest that this underworld, while totally devoid of form or shape, is still a space, a "haunt," an almost sacred spot filled with the presence of awesome power. Since, in terms of Wordsworth's metaphors, there is nothing to be *seen* in this haunt—no palpable shape upon which the mind can establish a purchase—reflexive consciousness discovers no limiting contours to its introspective plunge and thus finds itself upon a fearful journey into an open-ended abyss.

This kind of interior space is quite different from the confining space of Locke's *camera obscura.* This earlier metaphor for the mind reflects both Locke's rejection of the theory of innate ideas, which were often described by the Cambridge Platonists as kinds of inner light, and his restriction of the sources of knowledge to the not always certain reports of the senses.[8] Wordsworth's metaphor of the mental abyss, however, intimates a theory of the mind which goes far beyond Locke's careful empiricism. For immanent throughout the poet's interior space is the numinous power of the imagination —sometimes referred to by him as a mist or vapor, sometimes as a stream, sometimes as nothing more than the sound made by an unseen stream. In Book XIV of *The Prelude,* for example, Wordsworth characterizes his history of the growth and development of his imagination as the tracing of a "stream / From the blind cavern whence is faintly heard / Its natal murmur." [9] Earlier in the same book, where Wordsworth discovers in the mountain vision (also a vision of depths) from the top of Snowdon a "perfect image of a mighty Mind," he sees in a "blue chasm" in the outspread mist below a "breach / Through which the homeless voice of waters rose." And in this "dark deep thoroughfare," he goes on, "had Nature lodg'd / The Soul, the Imagination of the whole." [10] We note in these lines, incidentally, a suggestion of the same oxymoron of home / homeless —the "vagrant dwellers" of the "houseless" woods, the something's "dwelling" ubiquitously—which we saw in "Tintern Abbey": here the "homeless voice of waters" is "lodg'd" as an auditory emblem of the "Imagination" in the "blue chasm" in the mist.

In Book VI of *The Prelude,* after Wordsworth describes his discovery of having crossed the Alps without realizing it, the poet is suddenly confronted directly by his imagination:

> here the Power so called
> Through sad incompetence of human speech,
> That awful Power rose from the mind's abyss

> Like an unfathered vapour that enwraps,
> At once, some lonely traveller.[11]

The imagery here is especially involved. Not only does the imagination rise from the by now familiar subjective abyss; but the mind itself, confronted suddenly by its immanent power, is enclosed (imagination "enwraps" the traveler) by the intensity of its reflexive awareness. Consciousness is both the container that in its depths contains imagination and, now that imagination has leapt forth from these depths, the contained. Imagination is described as this confining, enclosing mist because so potent is its abrupt intrusion into awareness that the phenomenal world is lost. As Wordsworth tells us a few lines later: "the light of sense / Goes out." [12] The phrase "light of sense" recalls of course the Lockean epistemology and his notion of the mental *camera obscura* into which sensation, as it were, beamed its message. But when this light is extinguished for Wordsworth, there is discovered by the poet an innate power of the mind undreamt of in Locke's philosophy.

This direct, unmediated confrontation with imaginative power is rare in Wordsworth. The poet's primary aim, he tells us in the preface to *The Excursion*, is to sing a "spousal verse" celebrating the marriage of his mind to nature.[13] Such a marriage would inevitably have to avoid a prolongation of that state of mind brought about when the light of sense has gone out, for this kind of awareness necessarily involves a break with nature, a divorce of consciousness from the phenomenal world. Nature, the chosen partner of Wordsworth's mind, demands that the light of sense be maintained. The obvious difficulty in meeting this demand—from the point of view of the metaphors we have been examining—is that his creative power, the power whereby he seeks to blend his mind with nature, includes a tendency to force Wordsworth's awareness back toward

the abysses of subjective consciousness, to halt and en-
wrap the mental traveler. The mind's awareness of its
own imaginative power tends to be the antithesis of its
awareness of nature. And even when the power discovered in the abysses of the mind has been somehow
synthesized with consciousness of nature, it threatens
always to destroy nature by its own exuberance. Wordsworth complains in *The Prelude:*

> Oh! why hath not the Mind
> Some element to stamp her image on
> In nature somewhat nearer to her own?
> Why, gifted with such powers to send abroad
> Her spirit, must it lodge in shrines so frail? [14]

In these lines we again see Wordsworth's concern
with a dwelling: his "spirit" of imagination is to "lodge"
in nature, however "frail" its "shrines" may prove to be.
(The lodges of nature are appropriately "shrines" because the imagination is a numinous power.) In these
lines we also see a metaphorical paradigm of how
Wordsworth attempts to solve the problem posed by
his scheme of marriage. Reflexive imaginative consciousness is to be mediated by an awareness of nature,
to be experienced *sub specie naturae.* The poet will
transfer ("stamp") onto nature the image of his mind
as a place wherein lurks an immanent power. Nature
now must become a dwelling, a lodge, a home, and also,
therefore, a place of immanence. We might say that the
sense of the abyss of the mind is converted into a sense
of the depths of nature, but of course nature exhibits
these depths only insofar as imagination has been sent
abroad, as it were, to deepen nature. As Hartman has
put it, in commenting upon Wordsworth's "obsession
with specific place," "consciousness of self" is to be
"buried in nature." [15] Consciousness allows itself to become aware of imagination's power by displacing that

power into a shrine (or lodge, or home, or house, and so on) in the phenomena supplied by the light of sense. This relationship between consciousness and nature is inevitably oxymoronic: the "homes" provided by nature, although limited in terms of their phenomenal surface, must simultaneously possess an immanent open-ended space adequate to the nature of the numinous power of imagination whose original dwelling-place was the infinite underworld of Wordsworth's mind. The poet's "natural mysticism," therefore, might be characterized as a consciousness of this underworld opening out beneath the surface of the natural world.

By now it should be apparent toward what conclusions about the opening landscape of "Tintern Abbey" this brief account of Wordsworth's metaphors of immanence is leading. The sense of interiors that so fascinates the poet in his composition of place is in fact a sense of his own creative power enclosed within nature. This sense of interiors, of something far more deeply interfused, is what Wordsworth's eye attempts to resolve as it scans a landscape shot through with unseen presence and as the landscape itself seems to dissolve into the pervasive green of the season. The gradual focus of his eye upon the "uncertain notice" of the wreaths of smoke, and then the passing of his mind beyond the reach of sight into the depths of the green woods where he postulates "vagrant dwellers" in the "houseless" forest and a Hermit sitting alone in a cave,[16] are actions that recall in a remarkably distilled and naturalistic fashion the metaphors of consciousness we have been tracing: the imagination as a mysterious vapor rising from the depths, the oxymoronic dwelling in an unconfined space, the mind as a cave wherein lurks a secret power. And just as in the Alps the imagination enclosed Wordsworth's awareness like a mist and extinguished the light of sense, so here the rising smoke from the depths of the landscape beckons Wordsworth beyond the phenomenal world into the immanence of the forest, into the underworld of his own mind.[17]

We now can analyze what Professor Martz has characterized as the "associative" understanding of Wordsworth's meditation. After the composition of place of the first verse paragraph, the poet turns away from a direct contemplation of his scene and begins to explore the significance for himself of the "beauteous forms" (l. 22) of the landscape, an exploration that brings him to thoughts of both his past and his future, and also to an encounter with "something far more deeply interfused."

The language of this exploration suggests a continuing sense of the mind as a kind of interior space, a space into which the poet seeks to sink, escaping from the "heavy and weary weight / Of all this unintelligible world" (ll. 39–40). For the most part this escape, this inward sinking, is mediated through a vision of phenomenal nature, a vision that requires sensation or at least the memory of sensation before the poet can turn inward upon himself. At the end of the fourth verse paragraph, phenomenal nature, the nature revealed through the "language of the sense," is described by Wordsworth as the "guide, the guardian" of his heart, and finally as the "soul" of all his moral being (ll. 108–111). This characterization suggests the poet's recognition of nature's role in restoring him to a sense of his own heart, his own soul—to a sense of what is most essentially inward in himself. That nature is granted the epithet "soul," as if Wordsworth were saying that nature at least in one respect was his very essence, is but another manifestation of his habit of displacing his own inwardness into nature. But this displacement turns out to be reciprocal: having transferred his sense of self into nature, Wordsworth finds that nature made immanent leads him back toward himself.

At the beginning of the second verse paragraph, we find an example of such a backward turning. After having surmised an unseen Hermit at the heart of the landscape, Wordsworth continues to move beyond the immediacies of the scene by directing his consciousness toward his past: he transforms his sense of a human presence enclosed in the woods into an explicit memory of himself "in lonely rooms, and 'mid the din / Of towns and cities" (ll. 25–26). The cave of nature becomes a room in London, the identity of whose inhabitant is now no longer disguised. The poet's envisaging of hidden solitude is converted, through a process of association, into an overt memory of his own past solitude. This transformation makes more understandable the grounds of the sense of pervading immanence of the opening landscape. Consciousness of self is lodged throughout the scene because, as Wordsworth's eye passes over it, he is simultaneously aware, however subliminally, of the previous encounters of his mind with the scene. There was a direct encounter in the year 1793, the time of his first visit to Tintern Abbey, and then a series of indirect encounters made possible by his recalling, through the agency of affective memory, the "beauteous forms" during the period between 1793 and July 13, 1798, the day of his return and his meditation. The landscape, therefore, so strangely immanent, is not simply being seen, but is being seen "again"—the word is repeated four times in the first twenty-two lines. And so it is filled with an implicit history of the poet's past conscious experiences with its forms. We might say that it is the richness of the sense of "being seen again" which is, as it were, spatialized into the immanencies of the scene. We might also say, from this point of view, that Wordsworth's image of himself in a lonely city room is an image that was, up to a point in the poem, buried in the unseen spaces of the landscape: one of his earlier undefined thoughts of "more deep seclusion." The image now becomes emergent and explicit.

The seclusion of the city, as Wordsworth remembers it, also was characterized by movements of consciousness describable in terms suggesting a movement into an interior. Since Wordsworth apparently found in the phenomena of the city nothing more than "many shapes / Of joyless daylight" (ll. 51–52)—an oppressive experience of the "burthen of the mystery" of things (l. 38)—he would turn for "tranquil restoration" (l. 30) to his memories of the phenomena of the landscape around Tintern Abbey. He tells us that he owed to these remembered forms

> sensations sweet,
> Felt in the blood, and felt along the heart;
> And passing even into my purer mind,
> With tranquil restoration.
> [Ll. 27–30]

The language of these lines suggests a movement of awareness from a purely sensory state ("sensations sweet / Felt in the blood"), to a state of more diffused emotion ("felt along the heart"), and finally to a state that seems to transcend the physicality of sensation and emotion. The "sensations sweet" are said to pass somehow "even" into Wordsworth's "purer mind," as if these sensations were penetrating a region of interior consciousness where sensation is not normally found. These lines become more intelligible if we take them as descriptive of a movement of consciousness, by means of a contemplation of the remembered "beauteous forms," from a state that is almost exclusively sensory to a state that, though dependent upon remembered sensation, is more enclosed, more self-contained, more inward than the state of sensory awareness in which consciousness is principally directed toward the remem-

33

bered objects of sensation. In other words, this description of sensations passing into Wordsworth's "purer mind" suggests a movement of consciousness implicitly analogous to the movement of the poet's mind described in the first verse paragraph: from the surface of phenomena (though in "lonely rooms," a remembered surface) to a sense of enclosed immanence. And this meditative recall by the Wordsworth of 1798 of his earlier acts of remembering continues the process of inwardly deepening consciousness implicit in the poem from its very inception.

An even more intense form of this kind of consciousness is delineated in the final lines of the second verse paragraph. Wordsworth claims that he owes to his memories of the "beauteous forms" "another gift, / Of aspect more sublime" (ll. 36–37). This "aspect" is a certain kind or power of vision (L. *aspectus,* a seeing, a looking, a power of vision), and is described in language intimating an encounter with an immanent presence. This encounter occurs in

> that serene and blessed mood,
> In which the affections gently lead us on,—
> Until, the breath of this corporeal frame
> And even the motion of our human blood
> Almost suspended, we are laid asleep
> In body, and become a living soul:
> While with an eye made quiet by the power
> Of harmony, and the deep power of joy,
> We see into the life of things.
>
> [Ll. 41–49]

Wordsworth shifts in these lines into the first person plural, a rhetorical heightening that seems to universalize the availability of the kind of vision he is describing: "we," all of us, are capable of such an "aspect," such a power of vision. But this shift in point of view also suggests that it is of the nature of this kind of encounter with "the life of things" to convert the sense of "I" into a sense of "we," to attenuate the awareness of the self as a single, isolated ego. Such an awareness is thus analogous to the poet's awareness later in the poem of a ubiquitous, all-pervading "something" that lies in the innermost space of all things, including the mind of man: all identities tend to be lost in the universally immanent "something." Here the "aspect more sublime," this vision of "the life of things," is, we note, a seeing "into." And the language describing the movement of consciousness toward the moment of such seeing "into" indicates an awareness that passes beyond bodily sensation ("we are laid asleep / In body") toward an intensity of inward vision ("and become a living soul"). The eye that then sees "into" is of course not the corporeal eye—that along with the body has been "laid asleep"— but the inward eye of meditative introspection, an eye that has been made tranquil by a "power / Of harmony" and a "power of joy" which, we also note, is "deep." This word that Wordsworth uses to describe the sense of joy accompanying his vision suggests not simply the intensity of the joy but, more importantly from the point of view of the poem's language of immanence, the interior of consciousness in which harmony, joy, and a vision "into the life of things" are to be experienced. Finally, we might observe that this "aspect" is "more sublime" than that state of awareness in which he felt "sensations sweet" passing into his "purer mind." The comparative form of the adjective tells us that *both* structures of inward consciousness described in the second verse paragraph are "sublime"— a characterizing term that appears elsewhere in the poem only in Wordsworth's account of a "sense sublime" of "something far more deeply interfused." We might say, therefore, that whatever else "sublime" awareness, or "sublime" intentionality, is in "Tintern Abbey," it seems to involve an act in which consciousness senses itself penetrating an interior. And implicitly,

35

we might also conclude, Wordsworth's surmise at the end of his composition of place of a hermit enclosed within the landscape is a movement of his mind toward sublimity.

What exactly is this "life of things" into which Wordsworth claims he has seen? The question cannot be easily answered, for Wordsworth's retrospective emphasis is almost entirely upon the *state* of consciousness which sees "into" rather than upon the intended *object* of that state of consciousness. It is this structure of awareness which he claims is one of the principal gifts of his memories of the "beauteous forms." Moreover, as the third verse paragraph tells us, while the poet is certain both of having undergone this visionary experience and of the "method" of moving toward such a vision, the precise content of that vision, the presumed encounter with the "life of things," is not so certain after all:

> If this
> Be but a vain belief, yet, oh! how oft—
> In darkness and amid the many shapes
> Of joyless daylight; when the fretful stir
> Unprofitable, and the fever of the world,
> Have hung upon the beatings of my heart—
> How oft, in spirit, have I turned to thee,
> O sylvan Wye! thou wanderer thro' the woods,
> How often has my spirit turned to thee!
>   [Ll. 49–57]

These lines come as a dramatic turn in the poet's meditative action. (In a note to the second edition of the *Lyrical Ballads*, Wordsworth claims that the poem roughly resembles an ode in its "impassioned music" and in "the transitions"; it might be said that here is an impassioned example of the "antistrophe," or the "turning against," of that form.) [18] Until this point Wordsworth's awareness—first as he scanned the scene, then as he recalled the quality of his retrospective encounters with the scene—had been growing progressively more inward. But now it appears as if the very language of his meditation—the very articulation of his deepest intuition—has triggered a seizure of doubt. Certitude is abruptly converted into the uncertainty of a hypothesis. It is not the experience itself which might be "a vain belief." Instead, the question is whether he can characterize this vision as indeed a seeing "into the life of things." That phrase, though ringing with an almost metaphysical assurance, is at the same time so vague and extensive in its reference as to be potentially meaningless. What exactly, Wordsworth suddenly seems to inquire, am I to make out of this "aspect more sublime"? Can I base such a sweeping claim on such a private experience? Wordsworth's perplexity here prefigures the later perplexity hidden in his use of the groping term "something" to designate the indwelling spirit of all the cosmos. The poet's deepest intuitions can make no clarifying appeal to traditional myth or to a discursively worked out set of dogmatic formulations. And as he leaves behind the concrete sources of these intuitions, his memories of the "beauteous forms" of the landscape of Tintern Abbey, and as he works his way through his memory of these memories toward a statement of his vision, his language grows progressively more abstract, more generalized, and finally, even to himself, dubious.[19]

Yet this experience of doubt is momentary. The "antistrophe" of the third verse paragraph almost as quickly becomes an "anti-antistrophe." Lacking the support of a traditional myth or dogma, Wordsworth again turns to the undeniable facts of his experience and finds support against his doubts by recalling the genuine solace of his memories when he was oppressed by the "fever of the world" in the midst of "joyless daylight." But this appeal to the past is simultaneously an appeal to the present and to the immediate locale of his meditation. For out of this new memory of his acts of

37

remembering, he apostrophizes the "sylvan Wye" flowing directly before him in the landscape. His appeal, in other words, combines the experiential testimony of both the past and the present. His second-person address to the Wye as "thou wanderer thro' the woods" evokes yet another image of immanence—but an image that draws the poet's eye back into the specific scene and recalls him from the wavering expressed in his suddenly intruding hypothesis. This return to the concrete as an anodyne for doubt is an action that the poet later formulates as a fundamental requirement of his consciousness: Wordsworth writes in lines 107 through 109 that he is "well pleased to recognize / In nature and the language of the sense / The anchor" of his "purest thoughts." An anchor, of course, achieves a purchase upon stability by sinking into the depths of the sea; and here Wordsworth stabilizes himself, escapes from the wavering hypothesizing of one of his "purest thoughts," by addressing his awareness to an immediately given image of an action proceeding through an interior.[20] Vision is to be preserved by an adhesion to sensation, and his eye returns to an image of the immanence of the woods.

At the end of the third verse paragraph, Wordsworth has thus completed an almost circular movement of his consciousness: from present to past back to present; from landscape to a history of the relationships of his mind to that landscape back to landscape; from outward awareness to inward awareness back to outward awareness. This circular movement might almost be compared to an exploration of Chinese boxes: Wordsworth "opens" the strangely immanent landscape and discovers himself in the "box" of a room in the city. He recalls, almost seems to reexperience, the exploration by his past mind (trapped within that city box) into the remembered "beauteous forms." Immanence leads to deeper immanence. At the moment of deepest penetration, there occurs a vision "into" something he terms "the life of things." And immediately, at this moment of climax, the lid of this ultimate interior slams shut, and Wordsworth is left wondering whether he is guilty of a "vain belief." His anxiety is dispelled, or at least he attempts to dispel it, by a return through his memories to the surface of the landscape. This action of consciousness is similar in part to that poignant moment of introspection in Book XII of *The Prelude* where Wordsworth also uses the language of immanence to delineate an intense moment of perplexing introspection:

> Oh! mystery of man, from what a depth
> Proceed thy honours. I am lost . . .
> . . . .
>   The days gone by
> Return upon me almost from the dawn
> Of life: the hiding-places of man's power
> Open; I would approach them, but they close.[21]

In "Tintern Abbey" Wordsworth's search into the depths of subjectivity, a downward and inward journey that seems to carry him to a sight of what Frye, as we have noticed, has called "the creative world" or the "place of the presence of God," is terminated by a scrupulous hypothesis. I have already suggested that one reason for the poet's sudden worry about a "vain belief"—as if a question of doctrine were at issue—was the fact that Wordsworth's poetic articulation of his vision, his rendering of his "aspect more sublime" into statement, exposed the vision to the kinds of questions that can be asked of any statement, but are especially likely to be asked of any affirmations about the "life of things." But perhaps a still more fundamental reason can be offered to explain Wordsworth's abrupt upsurge of anxious uncertainty. Perhaps his anxiety is a displaced, brief, and somewhat muted expression of the "fear and awe" that, according to his preface to *The Excursion*, he claims to experience when he approaches the "haunt" and "main region" of his song, namely, his own mind. Perhaps the "life of things" is the numinous presence in the creative underworld of his mind—a presence I have already called the power of "imagination" [22]—and his fearful turning for comfort to the "sylvan Wye" wandering through the woods is but another attempt to find a lodge for his imagination in the phenomena of nature. Going too far beyond, or rather within, these phenomena can lead to a "serene and blessed mood." But the "Holy"—the "life of things"—is also "awful," and can breed anxiety and confusion.

IV

In the fourth verse paragraph Wordsworth plunges again into the past, but to a time even prior to the period of his solacing introspection "in lonely rooms." The poet attempts a picture of what he "was when first" he "came among these hills," that is, on his walking tour of 1793 (ll. 66–67). But what he was in that year, at least as "Tintern Abbey" describes it, was essentially a certain structure of consciousness immersed in the depths of the phenomenal world, a mind almost totally one with nature. He claims that "like a roe" he

> bounded o'er the mountains, by the sides
> Of the deep rivers, and the lonely streams,
> Wherever nature led: more like a man
> Flying from something that he dreads than one
> Who sought the thing he loved.
>
> [Ll. 67–72]

We have here another image of depths ("deep rivers") and of seclusion ("lonely streams"). We also have a curious implication in the simile that concludes the passage: Wordsworth suggests through the comparative form of the figure that though his relationship to nature at that time might be compared to the pursuit by a lover (himself) of his beloved (nature), a better char-

acterization of this relationship is the simile of himself
as the pursued fearing and flying from an unknown
pursuer ("something"). But of course if the pursuer is
only a vague "something," how can this simile be taken
—as it indeed seems to offer itself—as delineating the
relationship between his mind and nature? That this
dreadful "something" was *not* nature, although at first
reading it might be taken as such, is indicated by line
70 which tells us that it was nature who "led" the young
poet, and therefore was in a certain sense at least not
"behind," the proper place for all pursuers. Perhaps
even the "thing he loved" cannot be taken to refer to
nature. These lines really do not provide enough to
solve the puzzle, and all we can safely infer is that at
this time Wordsworth's consciousness was a curiously
ambivalent and contradictory mixture of the sense of
being led (by nature), of the sense of his own loving
pursuit (of nature?) and, most strikingly and memo-
rably, of the fearful sense of being pursued—by "something." Perhaps it is his awareness of these riddles of his
past state of mind which prompts Wordsworth to say:
"I cannot paint / What then I was" (ll. 75–76).

What he paints instead is a picture of nature in which
the phenomena of the landscape are almost identical
with certain structures of consciousness:

> The sounding cataract
> Haunted me like a passion: the tall rock,
> The mountain, and the deep and gloomy wood,
> Their colours and their forms, were then to me
> An appetite; a feeling and a love,
> That had no need of a remoter charm,
> By thought supplied, nor any interest
> Unborrowed from the eye.
>
> [Ll. 76–83]

Wordsworth's language presents a world in which there
is no distinction to be made between his intentionality
and his intended objects. The "directions" of conscious-

ness at this time were totally equivalent to the elements of the landscape. These "forms" quite simply—and the equation is startling—"were" for Wordsworth an "appetite; a feeling and a love." Thus there would be no need for "any interest / Unborrowed from the eye." The simple act of sensation, the mere act of looking, would be sufficient to involve Wordsworth's awareness in a range of conscious experiences far richer than the experience of ordinary seeing. To see is not to produce an occasion for possible emotion; to see is in itself to feel emotion. Phenomena *are* feelings, and feelings *are* phenomena. And to hear a "sounding cataract" is directly to be "Haunted" by a "passion," as if the "sounding cataract" in itself were a certain structure of consciousness (the experience of a "passion") impinging upon awareness. This image of the "sounding cataract"—an image of a dislocated sound—I take to be another image of immanence: it is analogous to the "soft inland murmur" of line 4 in that because its source is unseen, it suggests something hidden away from sight, an interior behind the surface of phenomena. It is precisely this sense of an interior which enables Wordsworth to describe the "sounding cataract" as if it were in itself a structure of consciousness. For, as we have already seen, the sense of immanence is for Wordsworth the sense of his own mind hidden in the landscape. And insofar as phenomena convey this sense of immanence, he is made dimly aware, in this case "Haunted," by the underworld of his mind which he has displaced into nature.

The previously noticed riddles of Wordsworth's curious comparative simile can now be unraveled. Both the term "something" and the term "thing" belong to the poem's language of perplexity (the most obvious example of this language is of course the poem's only other "something," that which is "far more deeply interfused"). This perplexity, I have been arguing, relates to Wordsworth's reflexive consciousness of the activity of

his own mind; a consciousness that in Book XIII of the
1805 *Prelude* is the "highest bliss" of those poetic minds
whose

> consciousness
> Of whom they are [is] habitually infused
> Through every image, and through every thought,
> And all impressions.[23]

The precise source of Wordsworth's perplexity in "Tintern Abbey" is the fact that, though the meditation ex-
plores how his mind is immanent in nature, infused
through "every image" and "all impressions," he never
can quite bring himself to recognize this infusion. To be
sure, the landscape makes him think a great deal *about*
his mind, its transactions with itself and with nature in
the past, the present, and the future. But during this
"thinking about," which constitutes the action of the
meditation, Wordsworth does not seem *explicitly* to
recognize that the special resonance of his perceptions,
both in the present and in the chambers of memory,
derives from the fact that frequently these acts of perception are simultaneously acts of apperception; that
frequently the intended objects of his consciousness
tend to become indistinguishable from the intentionality, the direction of consciousness, which grasps them.
Apperception, the reflexive sense of the mind's activity,
is lodged in perception, and thus nature becomes immanent.

Now, as we also have seen, Wordsworth is afraid of
staring too directly at his mind—afraid of too unmediated an act of apperception. His mind is a "haunt," a
sacred region filled with a numinous presence, and thus
it fills him with awe and dread. But this mind that is
experienced as a "haunt," as the place of the "Holy," is
not the mind he thinks *about,* the mind he constitutes
as the direct object of his meditation; it is rather the
immediately "living" mind he encounters more or less

43

obliquely in the act of apperception. While the Wordsworth of 1805 may have decided this structure of consciousness was "highest bliss," the Wordsworth of 1793
was flying from "something" that he dreaded—in much
the same way a soul of an earlier tradition might flee
from the awful majesty of God.[24] And just as this soul
might also pursue his God with love, so the Wordsworth of 1793 was pursuing the numinous presence of
the underworld of his mind in a landscape where phenomena and structures of awareness were identical.
But, of course, as the comparative form of Wordsworth's
simile indicates, the sense of fear predominated. Perhaps the image of the "sounding cataract" haunting him
like a passion most adequately summarizes the paradoxical doubleness of Wordsworth's relationship to his
act of reflexive self-awareness infusing itself throughout
the phenomena of nature. To be haunted by a passion
is to be haunted by his love, his desire to encounter the
visionary underworld of creative power. And he is simultaneously afraid of this love, of staring too directly
into the awe-engendering underworld of consciousness
—an underworld from which, however, he cannot quite
turn his face away in the patent "deep and gloomy
wood" of Tintern Abbey.

The Wordsworth of 1798, looking back at this time
of "aching joys" and "dizzy raptures" (ll. 84–85), does
not quite know what to make of it ("I cannot paint"),
except finally to say it is "now no more" (l. 84). Certainly the immediate intensity of the 1793 experience is
past. But has the experience been completely lost or has
it simply been attenuated? The very power of the poet's
description of the experience suggests that, in the words
of the "Immortality Ode," in the "embers" of his memory
"Is something that doth live." [25] Perhaps the difference
between his consciousness of 1793 and his consciousness of 1798 can be metaphorically depicted as the difference between the sound of the "sounding cataract"
of the past and the sound of the "soft inland murmur"

44

of the present. In other words, attenuation, not total loss. For Wordsworth still senses the landscape as immanent, though it is no longer seen and at the same time felt as a structure of consciousness. At this point in his life, it appears, he has so deeply lodged his self-awareness inside nature, that when he encounters it, as he does again shortly in the so-called "pantheistic" lines of the fourth verse paragraph, he does not know what to call it—especially since this "something" is "far more deeply interfused" than any of the other immanencies of the poem.

We must look upon the metaphor of "dwelling" in these lines as not only Wordsworth's most succinct description of the relationship of his mind and nature—a metaphor of extraordinary tension, yoking into a single precarious focus unbounded objects of perception (sky, air, ocean) with an apperception ubiquitously interfused. The metaphor can also be taken as Wordsworth's most explicit attempt in the poem to define his strangely immanent "something." Kenneth Burke has observed, in *A Grammar of Motives*, that to "tell what a thing is, you place it in terms of something else. This idea of locating, or placing, is implicit in our very word for definition itself: to *define*, or *determine* a thing, is to mark its boundaries, hence to use terms that possess, implicitly at least, contextual reference." [26] That Wordsworth feels he has resolved his perplexity—using the entire universe as a vehicle for contextually defining the unrecognized immanence of his consciousness—is indicated by his surprising "Therefore" which begins the sentence immediately following his vision of the "spirit" that "rolls through all things" (ll. 100, 102). Why, we might ask, a "Therefore"? Is a hidden syllogism being brought to a finish? Why, suddenly, this rhetoric of resolution?

The answer seems to be that Wordsworth has convinced himself that he has uncovered a way out of his difficulties. His experience of transcendence, of the hid-

45

den "life of things," is not a "vain belief" so long as he can contextually define, mark the boundaries of, this experience by reference to the phenomena of nature—a strategy of definition which uses the "language of the sense." Nature will provide what traditional myth or religious dogma no longer provides: a way both of making intelligible the visionary world and of mediating its terrors. Wordsworth is "still / A lover of the meadows and the woods, / And mountains"—the polysyndeton of these lines (102–104) expresses the intensity with which he feels his solution—because these "beauteous forms" will continue to serve not only as vehicles of vision but even more crucially as the means of resolving the haunting perplexities of that immanent vision. In fact, of course, Wordsworth's "religion of nature" is a means of providing symbolic form to the underworld, darker and more chaotic than "lowest Erebus," which is opened by reflexive self-awareness. And his "Therefore" emerges from the practical reason, not the theoretical. For his solution is to be almost exclusively experiential, derived from the "language of the sense." But at least in one respect his "religion of nature" will be Pauline: his "God," like Paul's, is a hidden God, that is to say, hidden from the discursive eye of speculative reason.

3

The Extensions of Consciousness

I

IN A PASSAGE that, according to de Selincourt, was originally intended for inclusion in the Snowdon episode of *The Prelude*, Wordsworth speaks

> of a mighty Mind
> That while it copes with visible shapes hears also
> Through vents and openings in the ideal world
> The astounding chorus of infinity
> Exalted by an underconsciousness
> Of depth not faithless, the sustaining thought
> Of God in human Being.[1]

While not exactly the clearest poety, these lines, especially the last three, seem suggestively corroborative of the thesis of this essay. They describe the poetic mind at its highest pitch of exultant creativity, dealing with the "visible shapes" of the phenomenal world, and at the same time feeling an "underconsciousness," a not quite explicit "thought / Of God in human Being." What Wordsworth here strangely calls "underconsciousness," I have called, in the preceding chapter, the act of apperception. In this act the mind does not constitute its own nature or activity as a direct object of consciousness. It has instead only an "underconsciousness" —a more or less indirect sense of the mind's own activity as that activity permeates every act of perception. In "Tintern Abbey" Wordsworth seems both fascinated

47

and perplexed by the pressure of apperception stirring within the depths of his perception. This "underconsciousness" most explicitly surfaces in his encounter with a universally interfused and extended "something," and indeed seems to give him a powerful intuition, if not an explicit conception, "Of God in human Being."

The purpose of the next two chapters is further to contextualize and deepen this analysis of Wordsworth's "sense sublime" by relating it to certain English theories of the sublime. The similarities between the kind of experience discussed in these theories and the kind of experience celebrated in many passages of Wordsworth's poetry have been examined often by critics and historians of ideas.[2] Thus it is not gratuitous to assume that the specific "sense sublime" of "Tintern Abbey" can be similarly examined. But such an examination, if it is to be consistent with my argument, must be in accord with the orientation of my analysis of Wordsworth's visionary encounter. I must consider these historically given theories, not so much in their own terms but for their phenomenological implications. I must then try to show that certain of these implications are consistent with my understanding of Wordsworth's "sense sublime."

In this chapter, therefore, I examine the ideas of a few eighteenth-century English theorists who describe the experience of the sublime—what henceforth I call "sublime consciousness"—in metaphors implying a dramatic spatialization of the mind. Such theories—those, for example, of Baillie, Gerard, and Priestley—are obviously relevant to my argument, concerned as it is with identifying Wordsworth's universally extended "something." Burke is not mentioned, for his approach to the problem exploits no such metaphors.[3] Nor do I attempt a systematic or historically comprehensive summary of the theorists whom I do mention. I try instead, by concentrating upon what seem to be their commonplaces, to evolve certain phenomenologically oriented generalities that might be taken as descriptive of the fundamental structures of sublime consciousness. In a sense, I gather notes toward what might be called a phenomenology of the sublime—a phenomenology in terms of which we can recognize Wordsworth's "sense sublime."

But my primary intention in this chapter—and in the next where I concentrate upon Coleridge's ideas about the nature of sublime consciousness—is not simply to suggest a more sophisticated way of understanding Wordsworth's relationship to some aesthetic speculations of the eighteenth and the early nineteenth century.[4] In both chapters, after having evolved my phenomenological generalities, I use them as a heuristic context for an extended discussion of the whole problem of sublime consciousness in Wordsworth's theory and practice of poetry.

II

Ernest Lee Tuveson has observed that according to "eighteenth-century theories of the imagination, the contemplation of a physically vast object, or one suggesting vastness, somehow increases the physical extent of the mind. . . . Awareness, it would seem, occupies a room whose walls can be pushed back. Behind the concept lies a spatial image of the mind."[5] John Baillie, for example, in his *An Essay on the Sublime*, writes that "every Person upon seeing a grand Object is affected with something which as it were extends his very Being, and expands it to a kind of *Immensity*. Thus in viewing the *Heavens*, how is the Soul elevated; and stretching itself to larger Scenes and more extended Prospects, in a noble *Enthusiasm* of Grandeur quits the narrow Earth."[6] The same spatializing of the mind is repeated, albeit with more restraint of phrase, by Joseph Priestley: "The mind . . . conforming and adopting itself to the objects to which its attention is engaged, must, as it

49

were, enlarge itself, to conceive a great object." [7] Alexander Gerard, in his *An Essay on Taste,* is so bluntly literal in his presentation of the same idea that he sees no need for the qualifying "as it were" of Baillie and Priestley: "We always contemplate objects and ideas with a disposition similar to their nature. When a large object is presented, the mind expands itself to the extent of that object, and is filled with one grand sensation." [8] Even the fastidious prose of David Hume does not escape a trace of this metaphorical habit: " 'tis evident that the mere view and contemplation of any greatness, whether successive or extended, enlarges the soul, and gives it a sensible delight and pleasure." [9]

The tendency of these spatializing metaphors, if we choose to take them literally, is to bestow upon the mind what Descartes had declared to be the essential and distinguishing characteristic of matter alone, namely, extension. The mind, like a balloon of remarkable elasticity, expands and enlarges itself in order to accommodate the enormous extension of the "grand Object" under contemplation. If indeed this "grand Object" appears to be immense or infinite—as, for example, Newtonian space appeared to be to many eighteenth-century observers—then the expanding mind finds itself in the paradoxical position of trying to accommodate an object that finally can be apprehended or grasped only by an equally infinite extension of the mind. I say "paradoxical" because from the point of view of strict logic this accommodation would be impossible: that the mind might grasp, or somehow contain, the immensity of a "grand Object," its own extension must become slightly *more* infinite, and by definition there can be no such thing as one infinity of extension larger than any other. This paradox is embedded in the language of Addison's description of one of the "pleasures of the imagination": "Our Imagination loves to be *filled* with an Object, or to *grasp* at any thing that is *too big for its Capacity.* We are flung into

a pleasing Astonishment at such unbounded Views, and feel a delightful Stilness and Amazement in the Soul at the *Apprehension* of them." [10] How the imagination can "grasp," or achieve an "Apprehension" of, an "unbounded" object is really not explainable in spatial terms. The unbounded precisely as unbounded can never be contained no matter how capacious the container. Still, to testify that such an "Apprehension" does somehow occur, we have feelings of being "flung into a pleasing Astonishment" and of a "delightful Stilness and Amazement."

The moral of course is that we ought not take literally these metaphors of the expanding space of mind. They are intended to describe not the *nature* of the mind but the *experience* of consciousness when consciousness is directed toward the "larger Scenes and more extended Prospects" of nature. These metaphors in fact describe the mind as it is subjectively apprehended in the experience of the sublime, in the feeling of what Gerard calls "one grand sensation." But to use spatial metaphors to describe this experience is deceptive in that such language tends to visualize the process, to convert it into an object of sight, and hence to give the misleading impression that the mind itself is being seen from an external point of view.[11] The proper interpretation of these metaphors requires that we treat them as expressive of a subjective process that, like any subjective process, is quite invisible.

What, then, does it mean to say that the mind "expands" when confronting a "grand Object"? We might begin to construct an answer by proceeding from the already mentioned Cartesian premise that the "essence" of matter is extension; from, in the words of Ernst Cassirer, one of "the basic presuppositions of the Cartesian metaphysics," namely, that "the thing, the empirical object, can be clearly and distinctly defined only through its purely spatial determinations. Extension in length, breadth, and depth is the only objective predi-

cate by which we can determine the object of experience."[12] From the point of view of this presupposition, we might say that in the experience of sublime consciousness, in the confrontation by the mind with a "grand Object," there develops an awareness of the mind's having been granted the "only objective predicate" whereby to determine empirical objects, namely, extension in length, breadth, and depth throughout material space. Insofar as the mind is *felt* to expand, it is sensed as possessing an increasing amount of extension, as spreading itself outward into space. Thus it is sensed as developing in at least one fundamental respect a resemblance to matter that, despite the bewildering variety of its manifestations, always exhibits extension. In the experience of the sublime, there is developed a structure of awareness in which the radical Cartesian divorce between mind and matter is *felt* to have been overcome.[13] The mind, by subjectively sensing itself as extended, simultaneously senses itself *as if* it were an empirical object spread, like the material atmosphere, throughout space. In Coleridgean terms we might characterize this structure of awareness as one in which there occurs the potentiality of a mediation between subject and object, assuming in this case mind to be subject and matter to be object. The grounds of this mediation would of course be the phenomenon of the simultaneous possession by both mind and matter of the common attribute of extension. And in Wordsworthian terms, sublime consciousness seems to offer suggestive possibilities for the marriage of mind and nature, especially for a marriage by the mind to nature in its more extended prospects. These possibilities become clear if we remember that the extension of the mind throughout space tends to become infinite insofar as the "grand Object," to which consciousness is struggling to accommodate its capacity, is in itself unbounded. Consciousness thus moves into a state of potentially becoming aware of itself as an oxymoronic

psychical-empirical entity ubiquitously spread out through nature. Or, in the words of Gerard, the mind at the moment of sublime consciousness "sometimes imagines itself present in every part of the scene which it contemplates." [14] The potential gloss that these words of Gerard provide for my reading of Wordsworth's "sense sublime" needs, at this point, no elaboration, except the remark that at the dramatic moment of sublime consciousness in "Tintern Abbey" Wordsworth fails to recognize it is his own mind that is ubiquitously indwelling throughout the vistas of sky, ocean, and air.

It must also be said that sublime consciousness, precisely because it can "sometimes" in some way imagine "itself present in every part of the scene" under contemplation, runs the risk of a profound sense of dislocation. Addison, for example, writing on the pleasures of contemplating the Newtonian heavens, gives us a hint of this risk. He comments on how we can feel ourselves so "lost in such a labyrinth of suns and worlds, and confounded with the immensity and magnificence of nature" that the mind feels "her self swallowed up in the immensity of the Void that surrounds it." [15] We might say that sublime consciousness—though involving a sense by the mind of its own increasing extension and therefore a sense by the mind of itself as a quasi-empirical object—does not seem simultaneously to permit a Cartesian use of the newly acquired predicate of extension to define or determine the mind in the objective manner appropriate for an empirical object. The mind, in its encounters with sublimity, can become "lost" and "confounded," unable to define itself in terms of its "spatial determinations." It almost seems as if the very intensity of the sense of the spatialization of the mind carries within itself a potential sense of a kind of "aspatiality," of passing over into a dimension of being where no localization of the self is possible. Precisely because consciousness moves toward an awareness of its being "every-where," it paradoxically exposes itself

53

to the risk of an awareness of its being "no-where," of being "swallowed up in the immensity of the Void." "Sublime space," the phenomenological space created by the mind's sense of its own infinite extension, is thus quite different in its effects from Cartesian space. Though both spaces are extended, the extension of Cartesian space creates the potential for both the determination and the localization of an object. But the extension of sublime space, the space that is phenomenologically generated by the mind's sense of itself spreading outward, establishes the possibility of both the indetermination and the dislocation of a subject. It follows, then, that if this sense of dislocation becomes too intense, the subject moves toward an awareness of "transport"—a favorite word in commentaries on the sublime—of being carried quite away from the world of ordinary, always confining localizations. The subject moves toward an awareness of, in the words of Baillie, quitting "the narrow earth" altogether or, in the words of Wordsworth, of passing over into "strange seas of Thought, alone." [16]

And if at this point we accept the justice of equating Wordsworth's state of imaginative consciousness with the state of sublime consciousness, we can arrive at a richer understanding of Hartman's contention that imagination in Wordsworth exposes him to the terrors of "apocalypse"—to the phenomenological possibility of the destruction and loss of the world. Wordsworth's ambition to "lodge" his mind in nature's phenomena can be seen as an effort to conserve the world, as an antithetical attempt to localize a consciousness that, as it becomes imaginative or sublime, moves toward the possibility of becoming so profoundly dislocated that it can experience a sense of "transport" out of the ordinary world of things in their places. The irony of this frightening possibility is that it is set up initially by the mind's acquisition of a sense of coming to possess the "only objective predicate" of the world of matter,

namely, extension. The paradox of this structure of awareness can be stated even more sharply: too great a fusion by consciousness with the material world—too great an abolition of the sense of the dualism of mind and nature—can lead to a phenomenological destruction of that world. From the point of view of this paradox, the famous Fenwick note to the "Immortality Ode" takes on an added significance. There Wordsworth observes that as a child he "was often unable to think of external things as having external existence, and I communed with all that I saw as something not apart from, but inherent in, my own immaterial nature. Many times while going to school have I grasped at a wall or tree to recall myself from this abyss of idealism to the reality." [17] Wordsworth's grasping "at a wall or tree" can be seen as analogous to his later more explicit poetic ambition to "lodge" his mind in nature's phenomena: both are acts of localization and both are attempts to overcome the vertigo caused by an encounter with the open-ended space ("abyss") of consciousness. Both acts are attempts to avoid apocalypse.

Now if the sense of dislocation experienced by sublime consciousness threatens the sense of the loss of the ordinary world of things in their places, it also exposes the mind to radical alterations of the sense of its own identity. Cassirer has observed that each "single, real thing bears witness to its reality above all by occupying a segment of space from which it excludes everything else. The individuality of the thing rests ultimately on the fact that it is in this sense a spatial individual—it possesses a sphere of its own, in which it is and in which it asserts itself against every other reality." [18] If the sense of the individual reality of a thing is "above all" a function of its spatial identity, we might ask these questions: what witness is borne to the reality of a mind by the fact that as it senses itself expanding outward into space, it comes to occupy a "segment of space" that is not exclusive at all, but indeed universally

55

inclusive? What becomes of the spatial individuality of such a mind when its expanding "sphere" does not permit it to assert "itself against every other reality" precisely because its sphere is moving toward an inclusion of every other reality? Answers to these questions are suggested in Tuveson's observation that the radical alteration of the mind's sense of its spatial identity during the experience of the sublime is, according to eighteenth-century theorists of the imagination, a "means of making the mind godlike." [19] What other mind but a quasi-divine mind could be so universally inclusive? We must understand of course that the god, to which sublime consciousness can feel a resemblance, is neither the Jehovah of the Old Testament nor the Heavenly Father of the New. This god is rather like the peculiarly spatialized being suggested by Newtonian theology; the god necessarily immanent throughout all of space since he is a being who, in the words of the "General Scholium" of the second edition of Newton's *Principia, "constitutes* . . . space." [20] This god also resembles the "Being . . . boundless, unsearchable, impenetrable" who is apostrophized in Shaftesbury's "The Moralists" as the "active Mind, infus'd thro all the Space," an interfusing presence who "Unites and mingles with the Mighty Mass!" [21] In short, sublime consciousness, when interpreted in the light of certain eighteenth-century versions of the nature of divinity, is a structure of consciousness in which, through a violent alteration in the sense of spatial identity, the sense of a distinction between creator and creature is potentially overcome. The mind experiences itself as having expanded to a state of divinity. It may enjoy the exalting and "sustaining thought / Of God in human being."

And even if consciousness does not quite attain such a majestic alteration in the sense of self, there still seems to be in the experience of the sublime ample ground for self-congratulation. In fact, according to many theorists, one of the characteristic pleasures of sublime consciousness is the recognition, either explicit or implicit, that the mind is indeed capable of experiencing sublimity. This recognition in turn seems to lead to an improvement in one's self-esteem. Longinus, as is to be expected, was the first to take notice of this phenomenon, and no doubt established such notice as a commonplace for English commentators of the eighteenth century. He writes that the "soul is naturally uplifted by the truly great; we receive it as a joyous offering; we are filled with delight and pride as if we had ourselves created what we heard." [22] Of course Longinus is here speaking of the rhetorical sublime, or the sublime in writing. But we can, disregarding the occasion of the experience, still note that Longinus suggests a state of reflexive self-awareness, a looking inward with pride, even though this state of awareness, paradoxically enough, does not seem to exclude the theoretical recognition at least that what has occasioned the experience of sublimity was in fact created by someone else and that, in all justice, any self-congratulation belongs to that author alone.

In Baillie's *An Essay on the Sublime* the theme of the improvement in self-esteem is quite explicit, though not directly attached, as it is in Longinus, to the "truly great" in composition. Baillie assumes, along with Longinus, that pride of consciousness is a natural consequence of an encounter with sublimity, a consequence not necessarily dependent upon any subsequent rational analysis of the experience. (The least bit of rational analysis would of course dispel the grounds—the sense that "we had ourselves created what we heard"—of the Longinian "delight and pride" in the self.) Baillie's account is in the Lockean tradition of empiricism and even suggests, with unintentional irony no doubt, a certain passivity of the mind, as it is endowed through sensory impressions with a better recognition of its own active excellence. Thus Baillie writes that "vast Sensations give the Mind a higher Idea of her own

57

Powers," and that these sensations are given by "Vast Objects." [23] Baillie also goes so far as to establish the improvement in self-esteem as one of the necessary tests of genuine sublimity, and sees a newly acquired pride of consciousness as one of the specific traits of sublime consciousness. He observes that that "only can be justly called *Sublime* which in some degree disposes the Mind to an Enlargement of itself, and gives her a lofty Conception of her own *Powers.*" [24] Given Baillie's commitment to the use of metaphors of the mind's extension, it is inevitable that he explains the "*Exultation* and *Pride*" of sublime consciousness as emotions that "the Mind ever feels from the *Consciousness* of its own *Vastness.*" [25] And, to be sure, this exultation can sometimes be the result of the mind's recognition of its own approximation of the *extensio Dei.* Baillie writes that just as one of the "sublime *Attributes of the Deity*" is "*Universal Presence,*" so the mind, when "contemplating the Heavens" and taking in the "mighty *Orbs* of the *Planets,*" becomes consciously "present to a Universe" through its expansion; and thus can feel a "noble Pride" as it recognizes itself "nearer advancing to the *Perfections* of the *Universal Presence.*" [26] It would seem that Baillie's commitment to metaphors of the mind's extension also commits him to the proposition that the quantity of the mind's expansion is somehow a revelation of its quality; the bigger the mind's capacity for extension, the better that mind is.[27]

This proposition can easily be converted into a program for increasing the powers of the mind. Edward Young, in his *Night Thoughts*, writes that certain phenomena, such as starry night skies, which are "ample of dimension" or "vast of size" can "an aggrandizing impulse give"; and that "vast surveys, and the sublime of things, / The soul assimilate, and make her great." [28] In other words, the proposition that in matters of sublimity quantity of the mind's extension is a revelation of its quality is a proposition that suggests a certain path toward psychological progress: namely, the more the mind is exercised through an expanding confrontation with the "sublime of things," the better that mind somehow shall become. Sublime consciousness thus might be described as an experience in which the mind can improve not only its awareness of its own excellence but even the very object of that self-applauding awareness. Gerard writes how the mind "finds such a difficulty in spreading itself to the dimensions of its object, as enlivens and invigorates its frame." [29] And Hume, commenting upon the difficulty or "opposition" the mind faces in attempting to conceive a great object, observes that in "collecting our force to overcome the opposition, we invigorate the soul, and give it an elevation with which otherwise it wou'd never have been acquainted." [30] Especially is this true, according to Hume, when the consciousness attempts to move backward through a "great removal" in time to grasp the "relicts of antiquity": the mind "being oblig'd every moment to renew its efforts in the transition from one part of time to another, feels a more vigorous and sublime disposition, than in a transition thro' the parts of space, where the ideas flow along with easiness and facility." The greater difficulty of the "transition" backward through time is based, according to Hume, upon the phenomenological fact that "space or extension appears united to our sense, while time or succession is always broken and divided." [31]

Finally, we might note that Priestley connects the difficulty in achieving sublime consciousness with the special pleasures of the experience. To conceive a great object, Priestley writes, "requires a considerable *effort of the imagination,* which is also attended with a pleasing though perhaps not a distinct and explicit consciousness of the strength and extent of our own powers." [32] In other words, in the severe exercise of its capacity for expansion, the mind can indirectly and somewhat paradoxically experience its own straining but successful powers as a source of pleasure. We might also observe that Priestley's phrasing ("though perhaps not a distinct and explicit consciousness") suggests the possibility of a structure of awareness in which the subject becomes aware of itself *qua* subject, not constituting its activity as a direct object of thought, but experiencing itself, as it were, from within—through the very intensity of its activity. Sublime consciousness, precisely because of the difficulty in achieving such a structure of awareness, establishes the possibility of a vivid act of apperception.

III

The theme of sublime consciousness both as inducing a special kind of self-consciousness and as increasing, in some way, the powers of the mind is a theme that seems to be involved in Wordsworth's various descriptions of the development and the workings of the poetic mind. In *The Prelude,* for example, the poet sees a special formative virtue in the fact that the circumstances of his boyhood provided him with "early converse with the works of God," especially in a region "where appear / Most obviously simplicity and power." [33] Now if we remember that "simplicity" and "power" are, according to many eighteenth-century theorists, characteristic features of those natural phenomena most likely to produce a sense of sublimity,[34] we can interpret Wordsworth's praise of an "early converse with the works of God" as a tribute paid to a youth spent among nature's sublime forms. Thus it should not seem unusual that Wordsworth illustrates the advantages of this kind of "early converse" with a reference to a mountain:

> By influence habitual to the mind
> The mountain's outline and its steady form
> Gives a pure grandeur, and its presence shapes

The measure and the prospect of the soul
To majesty; such virtue have the forms
Perennial of the ancient hills.[35]

This passage subtly echoes a theme we have already examined at length: the way in which the extension of a sublime object is in some way transferred to the mind. Wordsworth's version of the theme, however, avoids an emphasis, which is found in many commentaries, upon the violence and the uniqueness of the experience. For Wordsworth the mind is given a sense of its own "pure grandeur" by an "influence habitual," a constantly recurring encounter with the mountain's "outline" and its "steady form." Sublime consciousness, Wordsworth suggests, is not necessarily a sudden intrusion into ordinary consciousness, accompanied by the profoundly felt emotions of abrupt astonishment and amazement. Such a consciousness is also—at least in the circumstances of his youth in the Lake Country—a structure of awareness that can be gradually elicited by nature. And in this respect it is as important for the mountain's "form" to be "steady" as it is for the mountain's "outline" to possess, and therefore be capable of conferring, "grandeur." The mind, habitually exposed to the *enduring* sublimity of such a phenomenon, thus comes to recognize itself as possessing, like the mountain, an "extension," not so much through space, but through time. The "virtue" or power "of the ancient hills" to alter self-consciousness resides in the special fact that these phenomenal "forms" are "Perennial." Through constant "converse" with these hills, through a deepening comprehension of their eternity—what Hume might call a grasp of infinite "succession"—the mind somehow grows into an awareness of its own enduring qualities, an awareness of how indeed the "soul" has a "prospect" of "majesty" precisely because the mind is eternal.[36]

In the manner in which he stresses the temporality of this process of self-recognition, Wordsworth goes far beyond Baillie's somewhat mechanical account of the origin of sublime self-consciousness. Baillie sees the awareness of the "vastness" of the mind as simply engendered by the "vast" sensations conferred by "vast" objects. But Wordsworth, eschewing here such a literal reliance upon spatial metaphors, chooses to emphasize the organicism of the process: the mind is not suddenly "expanded" into a certain kind of self-consciousness; rather, through a gradual assimilation of the sublime phenomena of nature, it comes to recognize these phenomena as almost paradigmatic of its own powers.[37] And these phenomena can be so paradigmatic because they elicit, in the act of being habitually apprehended, a consciousness of these powers.

In the first book of *The Excursion* Wordsworth describes an education at nature's hand of the mind of the Pedlar. This solitary and wandering figure, one of Wordsworth's alter egos in the poem, grew up among the Scottish "hills of Athol," surrounded by a landscape very similar to Wordsworth's Lake Country. He is characterized as one of the many

> Poets that are sown
> By Nature; men endowed with highest gifts,
> The vision and the faculty divine;
> Yet wanting the accomplishment of verse.[38]

Wordsworth tells us that this mute, yet not inglorious visionary many times as a child "saw the hills / Grow larger in the darkness," and in complete solitude "Beheld the stars come out above his head." In the midst of these sublime phenomena, Wordsworth observes, "the foundations of his mind were laid." At a very early age the Pedlar had

> perceived the presence and the power
> Of greatness; and deep feelings had impressed
> So vividly great objects that they lay
> Upon his mind like substances, whose presence
> Perplexed the bodily sense.[39]

Wordsworth here suggests that an early encounter with "great objects" leaves an indelible impression upon consciousness, especially with respect to its capacity to constitute phenomena through the powers of sensation. The sensory memory of these "great objects" enabled the Pedlar, "as he grew in years," to establish a comparative perspective on all subsequent objects of consciousness: "With these impressions would he still compare / All his remembrances, thoughts, shapes, and forms." [40] And out of this continual activity of comparing his haunting memories of "great objects" with subsequent phenomena,

> he thence attained
> An active power to fasten images
> Upon his brain; and on their pictured lines
> Intensely brooded, even till they acquired
> The liveliness of dreams.[41]

For Wordsworth, it thus appears, an early encounter with "the presence and the power / Of greatness" in nature can induce in a developing mind a capacity to endow phenomena with a visionary resonance. The impressions left behind by "great objects" become, as it were, constitutive forms of perception which can significantly alter the content of subsequent acts of sensation. This effect is even more clearly suggested in one of the early drafts of this account of the Pedlar's mental history. In these lines, which de Selincourt supplies in his edition of *The Excursion*, the "great objects" are described as having been impressed so vividly upon the child's memory that they become "almost indistinguishably mixed / With things of bodily sense."[42]

Of great importance in this history of a growing consciousness is Wordsworth's emphasis on how early exposure to nature's sublime phenomena triggers a process that finally enables a mind to regard subsequent phenomena as if indeed they possessed the "liveliness of dreams," as if in one respect at least they were a special kind of subjective event. Whether we take the "images" upon which the child "Intensely brooded" as images directly perceived in nature (such a usage is not uncommon in Wordsworth's poetry),[43] or as images conjured up out of the memory, the point is that as objects of consciousness, they come to *appear*, through their acquisition of the "liveliness of dreams," less and less as images *of* nature, significant for what they might mirror of an external world detected through ordinary sensation. Instead, they more and more appear to take on the character of images specially constructed by the mind itself—images resembling in their very vividness those kinds of psychic entities engendered by the mind in the intense subjectivity of the act of dreaming.[44] We might formulate the meditative transformation in this fashion: phenomena come peculiarly to appear as if they had their origin in the mind and were not necessarily to be found outside the mind, that is, in objective nature. The world of ordinary sensation takes on the character of a world that is dreamed. The objects of consciousness come to appear as functions of subjectivity, and as somehow therefore revealing the activity of mind.

It follows that in this structure of awareness, ultimately growing out of an early encounter with nature's "great objects," natural phenomena can simultaneously be seen *as* mental phenomena. Nature is brought to the edge of the "abyss of idealism." Wordsworth goes on to tell us of how the boy, spending "many an hour in caves

forlorn, / And 'mid the hollow depths of naked crags,"
could trace in the "fixed and steady lineaments" of these
phenomena "an ebbing and a flowing mind, / Expression ever varying!"[45] Wordsworth's description of this
paradoxical vision, in which the fixity of phenomena
seen *as* natural phenomena stands in opposition to, yet
is somehow blended with, the fluidity of these same
phenomena simultaneously seen *as* mental phenomena,
is subtly related, I believe, to a theme already discussed: how in the experience of the sublime there is
developed a structure of awareness in which the sense
of a distinction between mind and matter tends to be
lost. In Wordsworth's account of the developing consciousness of the Pedlar, the mediating force is not a
sudden experience of the mind's extension into "vastness," but the haunting memories of youthful encounters
with the sublime, with the "presence and the power /
Of greatness." These lingering impressions provide the
psychological foundation of a meditative process in
which nature's phenomena become expressive of mind
—can be seen *as* mind—while at the same time remain-
ing nature's phenomena in their "fixed and steady lineaments." Wordsworth's mediation is not accomplished
through the annihilation of matter, the loss of nature in
the "abyss of idealism." On the contrary, as in "Tintern
Abbey," a vision of mind is obtained by an explorer of
nature's immanent places: " 'mid the hollow depths of
naked crags."

Perhaps the culmination of the Pedlar's education at
the hand of nature occurs in the way nature corroborates the Christian doctrine of immortality. Commenting on the boy's youthful exposure to the Bible-centered
orthodoxy of the Scottish church, Wordsworth writes:

> Early had he learned
> To reverence the volume that displays
> The mystery, the life which cannot die.[46]

But, Wordsworth immediately goes on, the truth of the Book of God and its "written promise" of man's immortality is authenticated for the Pedlar by his direct experience with nature's sublime objects. For

> in the mountains did he *feel* his faith.
> All things, responsive to the writing, there
> Breathed immortality, revolving life,
> And greatness still revolving; infinite:
> There littleness was not; the least of things
> Seemed infinite; and there his spirit shaped
> Her prospects, nor did he believe,—he *saw*.
> What wonder if his being thus became
> Sublime and comprehensive! [47]

We can distinguish in this passage two related ways in which nature assists in the corroboration of the Christian doctrine of immortality. Both seem to involve the kind of self-consciousness evoked in the experience of the sublime. First, there is the corroboration of the article of faith by the *feelings* engendered in the Pedlar by his being "in the mountains." Wordsworth suggests that the written promise of God is in some way "Breathed" again by nature's phenomena. These phenomena speak, as it were, of "revolving life, / And greatness still revolving"; and buried in Wordsworth's twice repeated participle is the traditional symbol of eternity: the circle. Of course nature's testimony has to be understood as its power to elicit in the Pedlar certain feelings. These feelings, since they bear witness to the immortal nature of man's soul, can be characterized as feelings "about" the self or as a form of self-consciousness. We also note that the Pedlar's vision is directed outward, upon "All things" which are described as "responsive to the writing," that is, corroborating and answering to the Bible's promise of immortality. The precise nature of this act of corroboration thus can be understood as related to that characteristic of sublime consciousness already discussed: how the mind, in the act of apprehending sublime phenomena, comes to feel, explicitly or implicitly, the extent and nature of its own powers. In the act of comprehending the eternal greatness of the mountain landscape, the Pedlar grows aware of his own eternal greatness.

Not only is nature "responsive to the writing" of the Christian Bible, but the Pedlar himself actively answers to nature's initial responsiveness. Out of the structure of consciousness that nature's sublimity induces in him, the Pedlar becomes creative: "his spirit shaped / Her prospects, nor did he believe,—he *saw*." This shaping into visibility of man's immortal prospects can be distinguished as the second way in which the "written promise" is corroborated. The grounds of assent have moved from the word to the emotions to the eye. Not only does the Pedlar *believe* in his immortality, not only is he then given *feelings* of his immortality by nature's phenomena, but indeed, through his own creative response, he finally comes to *see* in nature's phenomena an image of his immortal nature. Sublime self-consciousness is displaced into nature and therefore becomes visible. The eternity of mind is seen under the aspect of nature: the eternity of the mountains is sensed as an image of the eternity of the self. And in turn faith, which according to Saint Paul is the substance of things unseen, is no longer necessary: "nor did he believe." The Pedlar moves beyond the necessity of faith because his intuition of his own nature takes on the character of an empirical act, a sensory encounter with an externally existing objective world. Apperception, prompted by perception, is "shaped" back into perception.[48]

IV

In his account of the Pedlar, Wordsworth suggests a very close relationship between sublime self-consciousness and the activity of the imagination, almost as if such a structure of consciousness were the source of imagination's operations.[49] This connection is quite explicitly made by Wordsworth in his "Preface to Poems (1815)." There, discussing the shaping and creative functions of the imagination, the poet writes that that power finds its greatest "delight" in the acts of "consolidating numbers into unity, and dissolving and separating unity into number." Wordsworth goes on to observe that these actions are "alternations proceeding from, and governed by, a sublime consciousness of the soul in her own mighty and almost divine powers."[50] Without at this point going into the question of what Wordsworth exactly means by his description of imagination's operations of consolidating numbers into unity and of dissolving unity into numbers, it is important to note that both transformations, or "alternations," find their source for Wordsworth in an act of self-consciousness which he designates as "sublime." It is equally important to note that we cannot logically assume this special structure of consciousness to have been produced initially by the mind's awareness of its imaginative activity (though, to be sure, such an awareness may augment the sense of self as sublime); for Wordsworth explicitly tells us that imagination's activity *proceeds from*—almost as an effect proceeds from its source —sublime self-consciousness. Thus—and this is crucial to observe—we cannot assume that when Wordsworth speaks of the "mighty and almost divine powers" of which the mind becomes aware in the creative act, he is necessarily referring exclusively to the powers of the imagination to consolidate and to dissolve. It would seem that the mind becomes reflexively aware of its powers in a different, perhaps more inclusive way; that it is out of this initial and "sublime" self-awareness that imagination arises and proceeds to the delightful labor of shaping and creating "alternations" in phenomena. How, then, are we precisely to understand the relationship between imagination and sublime self-consciousness?

In his "Preface to Poems (1815)" Wordsworth speaks about the "grand storehouses" in literature "of enthusiastic and meditative Imagination." These "storehouses" (the metaphor is another example of Wordsworth's preoccupation with dwelling-places) are "the prophetic and lyrical parts of the Holy Scriptures, and the works of Milton; to which I cannot forbear to add those of Spenser." Wordsworth explains that he selects these writers "in preference to those of ancient Greece and Rome, because the anthropomorphitism of the Pagan religion subjected the minds of the greatest poets in those countries too much to the bondage of definite form; from which the Hebrews were preserved by their abhorrence of idolatry. This abhorrence was almost as strong in our great epic Poet, both from the circumstances of his life, and from the constitution of his mind. However imbued the surface might be with classical literature, he was a Hebrew in soul; and all things tended in him towards the sublime." [51]

Wordsworth's reasoning in this passage seems based upon a provocative series of equations. Reading these backward, we might first say that to have a mind like Milton's, which tends "towards the sublime," is to be a "Hebrew in soul." But to be a "Hebrew in soul" is to have an "abhorrence of idolatry." And to have an "abhorrence of idolatry" is not simply to reject the "anthropomorphitism of the Pagan religion," but more generally it is to have a mind that refuses to be "subjected . . . to the bondage of definite form." Telescoping these equations, we might then say that, according to Wordsworth, a mind that like Milton's tends "towards the sublime" is a mind that in its intentionalities tends to go beyond the limitations or the "bondage" of any "definite form." Consciousness tending toward the sublime experiences the freedom of having the indefinite as its direct object of awareness.

Sublime *self*-consciousness thus appears to be for Wordsworth an act in which the self becomes conscious of the self without being "subjected . . . to the bondage of definite form"; the self becomes aware of the self as nothing more precise than a "something," as an entity neither defined for consciousness in any fixed conceptual way nor delineated for consciousness by means of any specific, in-forming image. Sublime self-consciousness involves an intuition of the self *without* a principle whereby this self-awareness might be limited, either by a concept of the self or by an image of the self. Translating this structure of consciousness into grammatical terms, we might say that it is a self-awareness that lacks a predicate complement. The fact of the self's reality is apperceived, its presence and existence are intuited; but this fact is in no way limited by any simultaneously grasped and defining assertion about the nature of the self: "I am," but not "I am x" or "I am y." The Coleridgean echo here is not accidental, for in this structure of awareness we have a perfect fusion of subject and object. Just as consciousness cannot limit its awareness of self through a concept or an image, so it cannot constitute itself as a distinct object of thought through a concept or an image. The self is present to the self in a thoroughly unmediated fashion. Minds that possess the potential for such a structure of awareness are, in Wordsworth's terms, "truly from the Deity, / For they are Powers." They possess a "consciousness / Of whom they are" which is "habitually infused / Through every image, and through every thought, / And all impressions." [52] These minds also possess an almost godlike liberty, for as long as they remain in such a state of self-awareness, they will never find their self-consciousness subjected to the bondage of any definite image, or confining thought, or restricting impression. Latent in any specific act of sensation will be the indefinite reality intuited in the act of apperception, the sublime presence of a nearly divine "something" universally interfused.

It should, therefore, not be surprising that sublime

self-consciousness is sometimes described by Wordsworth in metaphors suggesting an encounter with
a completely blank, thoroughly open-ended space: a
plunge into the "abyss of idealism" or a glimpse into a
"haunt" that is a "blinder vacancy" than the mytho-
logical "Chaos" or the "darkest pit of lowest Erebus."
These metaphors of self-consciousness are directly in
the tradition of those metaphors of the mind's infinite
expansion so frequently used in the eighteenth-century
commentaries on the sublime. Both sets of metaphors
are expressive of a dissolution of the mind's sense of
itself as a fixed and limited entity.[53] Both sets of metaphors are also expressive of the vertigo of sublime self-
consciousness, a vertigo brought on by the intrusion
into awareness of a sense of the mind's "mighty and almost divine powers."

Nor, finally, should it be surprising why imagination,
according to Wordsworth, "recoils from everything but
the plastic, the pliant, and the indefinite."[54] In this
act of recoil, imagination shows that it is indeed "governed by" a "sublime consciousness of the soul" of its
own undefined and therefore unlimited nature. In this
act of recoil, imagination, reflecting the structure of
awareness in which it finds its origin, refuses to submit
the mind's freedom to the bondage of definite form. It
is the power whereby the mind does not lose its undefined sense of self in any act of specific perception. It
enables the mind to sustain and marry its undefined
sense of self with the phenomena provided by nature;
these phenomena become immanent and are filled, as it
were, with sublime self-consciousness. Consciousness of
nature is thus filled with "under-consciousness." The
Wordsworth of "Tintern Abbey" discovers the most intense fruition of imagination's mediating power in his
encounter with a "something" indwelling throughout
the vast expanses of sky and ocean. The Pedlar of Book
I of *The Excursion* shapes his intuition of his immortal
nature into the visibility of the sublime landscape of
the hills of Athol.

4

The Intuition of Existence

SAMUEL TAYLOR COLERIDGE has not bequeathed to us a perfectly developed theory of the sublime. We must instead be content with what he has scattered throughout his often fragmentary work: a legacy composed of a number of extraordinarily provocative comments that at times seem to be suggestively involved with his deepest researches into the nature of the mind and the power of the imagination.

In this chapter I consider these random speculations of Coleridge, not so much to pull them together into an appearance of consistency and encompassing range —an appearance that they do not perhaps deserve— but to explore the ways these speculations might deepen our understanding of sublime consciousness in Wordsworth.[1] I mediate between the theory of Coleridge and the practice of Wordsworth in much the same way I have already mediated between theory and poet: by considering Coleridge's speculations, not so much in their own terms but for their phenomenological implications. I then ask whether these implications corroborate the description of Wordsworth's visionary act so far developed in this essay.

Precisely because of the fragmentary nature of Coleridge's ideas on the sublime, these implications can be pursued only with special rigor and clarity. Coleridge, even in his fragments, is too subtle a thinker to be dealt with glibly. And if I wish to locate and extend my analysis of Wordsworth's "sense sublime" in a phenomenological context extrapolated from Coleridge, I must exercise caution that this context not be gratuitously established. Hence the chapter that follows is lingeringly argumentative and analytical—and more about Coleridge than about Wordsworth. Only in the last two sections do I turn back to Wordsworth and there attempt to suggest, through explications of two passages from *The Prelude*, that what Coleridge calls the "metaphysical Sublimity" of the ego is for Wordsworth the ultimate source of his transforming act of the imagination.

II

Just as many eighteenth-century theorists of the sublime argue that sublime consciousness is induced in an attempt by the mind to "comprehend" or "grasp" something that is too large for its capacity (the infinite space of the Newtonian heavens, for example), so Coleridge sees sublime consciousness as involving an encounter between the mind and, in the words of Clarence Dewitt Thorpe, a "form [which] escapes successful apprehension."[2] In his marginal notes to Herder's *Kalligone*, Coleridge remarks that a "whole (a visual whole, I mean) . . . cannot be sublime. A mountain in a cloudless sky, its summit smit with the sunset, is a beautiful, a magnificent object: the same with its summit hidden by clouds and seemingly blended with the sky, while mists and floating vapours [encompass it, is sublime]."[3] Coleridge's point seems to be that it is not the vastness as such of the mountain which occasions the experience of sublimity. Instead, it is the fact that the perceptual boundaries of the mountain are obscured which allows for the experience and permits him, as an aesthetician concerned with the precise use of terms, to designate the mountain as "sublime." It seems that for Coleridge the intended object of sublime consciousness must be in some way undefined, lacking in observable limits, and therefore not exhibiting a precisely delineated spatial identity. Such an object may not, in the words of Cassirer, "bear witness to its reality . . . by occupying a segment of space from which it excludes everything else." [4] On the contrary, its status as the intended object of sublime consciousness involves an experience of a space which is open-ended. Or as Coleridge puts it in one of his numerous attempts to distinguish the beautiful from the sublime: "Nothing not shapely . . . can be called beautiful: nothing that has a shape can be sublime except by metaphor *ab occasione ad rem.* So true it is, that those objects whose shape most recedes from shapeliness are commonly the exciting occasions." [5]

Coleridge indicates that he found a number of such "exciting occasions" in the gloomy and receding spaces of the Gothic cathedral. He observes that "Gothic art is sublime. On entering a cathedral, I am filled with devotion and with awe; I am lost to the actualities that surround me, and my whole being expands into the infinite; earth and air, nature and art, all swell up into eternity, and the only sensible impression left is, 'that I am nothing!'" [6] Among the extraordinarily rich and even puzzling implications of this passage is, first, the notion that this experience of the sublime depends upon a situation—an architecturally enforced and controlled obscurity—in which shapes tend inevitably to recede from shapeliness. Second, the "actualities" of the cathedral, as they recede from shapeliness, can no longer "bear witness" to their reality by occupying an excluding and exclusive segment of space; they thus become "lost" to the observer. He can overlook—simply, in some way, look beyond—these "actualities" insofar as they appear spatially diffused and open-ended. Their identity, as it were, pours out through the gaps in their spatial boundaries. Third, the dissolution of the spatial identities of the objects of perception seems to lead to a dissolution of a sense of a fixed spatial identity on the part of the subject. To the extent these objects or "actualities" phenomenally dissolve into the Gothic gloom, they no longer "surround" the subject and thus no longer provide a means whereby he might generate a sense of his own spatial exclusiveness and identity. By becoming "lost to the actualities that surround" him, he also loses his sense of the way in which his presence is delimited or defined in space. Hence the subject can feel his "whole being" expanding "into the infinite." It is now his turn to feel his spatial identity, as it were, pouring out through the gaps created in his spatial boundaries.

Obviously, Coleridge's use of the term "expands" echoes the habit of eighteenth-century theorists to speak of consciousness in spatial metaphors. Indeed, Coleridge's use of the metaphor seems to suggest the same phenomenon spoken of, in one way or another, by these theorists—namely, that sublime consciousness involves a radical alteration in self-consciousness. One way of characterizing this alteration is to say that the self now becomes aware of itself, potentially at least, as deserving to be designated as "sublime" according to the way in which Coleridge himself insists the term be applied. Insofar as the self feels itself expanding "into the infinite," quite obviously it senses itself as approaching, in some metaphoric way, a state in which it may no longer sense itself as in any way possessing a "shape." The notion of an infinite shape, like the notion of an enclosed infinite space, is a contradiction in terms. Thus, by sensing itself as having expanded into infinity, the self will have fulfilled one of the necessary conditions for a Coleridgean designation of itself as "sublime": it will have developed a sense of itself as having infinitely receded "from shapeliness."

Another way of characterizing this alteration in self-consciousness is to say that it seems to include a growing sense of the self's becoming, in one fundamental respect, identical with what is not the self: "all swell up into eternity." Subject and object can become one in the act of swelling into eternity because, from a phenomenological point of view, both subject and object no longer possess a delimited spatial identity. Precisely because the phenomenal space of both subject and object does *not* exclude everything else, a potential is established for consciousness whereby the mind might sense everything as merging into or including everything else. Thus a structure of awareness is induced in which contraries can be resolved: not only do subject and object become one through corresponding losses of their spatial exclusiveness and identities (from the point of view of the observer in the Gothic gloom), but even "earth and air, nature and art" can move toward a reconciliation of their traditional conflicts insofar as these phenomena become caught up in a consciousness by the self of itself expanding "into the infinite." It would seem, therefore, that sublime consciousness for Coleridge—at least the kind of sublime consciousness provoked in him on "entering a cathedral"—is a structure of awareness in which phenomena tend to undergo the same sort of changes that, according to the theory of the *Biographia,* they undergo when exposed to the esemplastic power of the imagination: they are dissolved, diffused; and phenomenal contraries move in some way toward reconciliation.

Finally, the passage suggests that for Coleridge the experience of the Gothic sublime confines the range of awareness to nothing but self-consciousness—and that of a very special kind: "the only sensible impression left is, 'that I am nothing!'" Since Coleridge indicates that this "only sensible impression" is the culminating intensity of his whole encounter with Gothic sublimity, we are free to characterize this sense of the self's nothingness as a version of sublime self-consciousness. This state thus seems to be reached by a simultaneously centrifugal and centripetal action: the sense of the self centrifugally expanding "into the infinite" is accompanied by a centripetal constriction of awareness to the self alone, indeed to a self of which there is finally no predication possible beyond the term "nothing." [7]

And now of course we are struck by a paradox. How can a sense of the self expanding "into the infinite" develop at the same time into a sense of the self as "nothing," as if the self were annihilated? Why does Coleridge not go the way of so many eighteenth-century theorists and characterize the culminating intensity of sublime self-consciousness as a kind of apotheosis, an exhilarating sense of the mind's quasi-divine power and capacity as it comes to resemble the deity diffused through the infinite reaches of Newtonian space? Why instead does he use language that could be taken to indicate a kind of self-awareness at the furthest possible remove from such sublimity? That this expansion occurs within the gloomy space of a Gothic cathedral hardly accounts for the paradox; its resolution must be sought by looking at some of Coleridge's other comments on the sublime.

III

In one of his essays for *The Friend,* Coleridge lays down the postulate that "deep feeling has a tendency to combine with obscure ideas, in preference to distinct and clear notions." He goes on to speak of certain "deep feelings which belong . . . to those obscure ideas that are necessary to the moral perfection of the human being." And he insists that these feelings ought to be reserved "for objects, which their very sublimity renders indefinite, no less than their indefiniteness renders them sublime,—namely, to the ideas of being, form, life, the reason, the law of conscience, freedom, immortality, God." [8] Coleridge here suggests that the experience of the sublime is derived from an encounter with obscurity and indefiniteness. Such an encounter is also the occasion of "deep feelings," which presumably cannot be so successfully occasioned by whatever is "distinct and clear." [9] Coleridge here postulates for the world of ideas what we have already seen him postulating for the world external to the mind: the proposition that "nothing that has a shape can be sublime," and this proposition's corollary that "those objects whose shape most recedes from shapeliness are commonly the exciting occasions." Of course an idea cannot be said to have a "shape" if we take the term to apply exclusively to the physical contours of an object. But by an easy and obvious metaphoric extension, an idea can be said to have a "shape" insofar as it possesses the Cartesian virtues of clarity and distinctness. Conversely, therefore, to the extent that an idea becomes obscure and indistinct, it takes on a metaphorical resemblance to those objects in the physical universe "whose shape most recedes from shapeliness." And just as these shapeless objects (a cloud-draped mountain, for example) are "exciting occasions" of sublime emotion, so certain obscure and indistinct ideas (the idea of God, for example) have "a tendency to combine" with "deep feelings."

Most worthy of notice in this passage, however, is Coleridge's suggestion of a reciprocal relationship between the quality of being indefinite and the quality of being sublime. He says that not only is it the "indefiniteness" of certain ideas that "renders them sublime," but also it is "their very sublimity" that "renders" them "indefinite." We can generalize from Coleridge's statement of this reciprocity the proposition that for him the kind of "indefiniteness" he proposes as a necessary characteristic of the sublime object (whether this object be an idea or something in the external world) is not necessarily a characteristic of that object taken in itself. Rather, this "indefiniteness" is largely a function of the relationship between subject and object, or between thinker and idea, or between observer and observed.

Whenever anything is grasped as sublime, it necessarily takes on the characteristic of appearing "indefinite," whether or not it possesses this characteristic in itself apart from any relationship to a subject. The quality of "indefiniteness" possessed by the sublime object thus might be exclusively phenomenal, an "appearance" constituted by the way in which that object stands in relationship to the subject. And when we find Coleridge categorically stating that "nothing that has a shape can be sublime," we perhaps best understand him as saying that nothing can be sublime that cannot, in some way, be made to take on a kind of phenomenal shapelessness or indefiniteness.

All this suggests that for Coleridge the true source of the sublimity of anything, physical object or idea, is always the subject. Thus he writes: "I meet, I *find* the Beautiful—but I give, contribute, or rather attribute the Sublime. No object of Sense is sublime in itself; but only as far as I make it a symbol of some Idea. The circle is a beautiful figure in itself; it becomes sublime, when I contemplate eternity under that figure." [10] We can easily see, from the point of view of Coleridge's previously cited distinction between the beautiful as necessarily shapely and the sublime as necessarily shapeless, why the circle can be taken by him as a "beautiful figure in itself." The circle is *found* to be, of and by itself, a figure of exact proportions. But how this same circle can also become sublime for Coleridge is not so immediately evident. Clearly the circle, even as symbol of the idea of eternity, remains an eminently shapely figure in a purely objective sense. We can resolve this problem if we understand that Coleridge's use of the term "shape," in the proposition that "nothing that has a shape can be sublime," finally refers not to the objective shape of a thing but rather to the phenomenal shape a thing may assume when regarded by the subject from a certain point of view. The circle, precisely because of its function as a symbol of the idea of eternity, is now involved with an idea that Coleridge would regard as "obscure" and "indefinite"—and therefore sublime. The circle, though retaining its purely objective shape, does indeed recede from shapeliness to the extent that it comes to function as a phenomenon symbolic of the obscure and indefinite idea of eternity. For consciousness, the image of the circle as objectively shapely recedes, as it were, into the obscurity of the idea of eternity. The circle comes to be seen not for what it is, but for what it represents as a symbol; as a phenomenon, therefore, its objective shape sinks away into the indefiniteness of its symbolic dimension. It takes on a kind of subjective shapelessness, and thus is rendered sublime.[11]

Thus, in facing the question of what exactly Coleridge means when he speaks of attributing the sublime to an object of sense, we might say that the object must somehow become caught up in a purely subjective awareness of something obscure, indefinite, shapeless. Consciousness bestows upon that object of sense an appearance that in fact has been generated in a purely subjective encounter. Sublime consciousness is somewhat Janus-faced: though directed outward toward a sublime object in the external world, it is simultaneously directed back toward the self, toward a source of obscurity and indefiniteness discovered within the realm of subjectivity.

It follows that the sublime in literature is essentially a record of a poet's subjectivity. All poems, even epics, insofar as they are taken as sublime poems, are at the same time being taken as expressive documents, revealing the inner history of the poet's mind. Thus Coleridge can write that in *"Paradise Lost* the sublimest parts are the revelations of Milton's own mind, producing itself and evolving its own greatness; and this is so truly so that when that which is merely entertaining for its objective beauty is introduced, it at first seems a discord."[12] *Paradise Lost,* from this Coleridgean point of view, is to be read as a document allowing all to see Milton's mind in the act of discovering the sources of sublimity within itself. When the poem is so read, the discovery of images of "objective beauty," presumably images possessing the quality of shapeliness, appears at first glance to be at odds with the poem's projection of the obscurity and indefiniteness of Milton's own sublime subjectivity. Also, we might note, Coleridge regards Christianity as especially conducive to sublime consciousness because it provides a way of thinking about reality whereby "the Imagination is kept barren in definite Forms and only in cooperation with the Understanding labours after an obscure and indefinite Vastness." [13] Sublime consciousness thus seems to be for Coleridge a structure of awareness in which all conceptions tend to recede from shapeliness, and the mind is left groping in the darkness of its own subjectivity for an "indefinite Vastness."

The question must now be asked in what way the subject can attribute the sublime, not to an object of sense, but to those "objects" of the world of ideas, that is to say, to ideas themselves. Earlier, in explaining how a distinctly shaped object of sense such as a circle can be rendered sublime, I argued that the phenomenal shape of the circle, as it comes to function as a symbol of the idea of eternity, sinks away, as it were, into the obscurity of its own symbolic dimension. This analysis assumes that the subjective source of the sublime in this instance is the idea of eternity as such; that such an idea is inevitably indistinct and therefore sublime. But might it not be more accurate to locate the subjective source of the sublime, not so much in the ideas that are entertained by sublime consciousness but in the very *way* in which sublime consciousness "labours after" such indefinite ideas? Might it not be more precise to regard the subjective source of the sublime, not as an encounter by the mind with certain of its own ideational contents (ideas of eternity, God, immortality, and so on) but as an encounter with its own subjective action in attempting to come to terms with such ideas? I am arguing that the subjective source of the sublime is in fact an act of

81

apperception in which consciousness becomes vividly aware of itself because of its inability to define its intentionality, or direction of consciousness, with respect to any precisely delimited conception or idea. Consciousness, laboring after the "obscure and indefinite Vastness" suggested by such an idea as the idea of God, is thrown back upon itself, becomes self-conscious with respect to its own laboring. Precisely because of its inevitable failure to achieve the "rest" or stasis of a perfectly adequate image or conception of an "obscure and indefinite Vastness," consciousness becomes vividly aware of itself as an indefinitely dynamic agent, as possessing an intentionality in pursuit of an intended object which infinitely recedes from adequate comprehension. Sublime consciousness for Coleridge reveals itself to be, in the last analysis, sublime self-consciousness, and those ideas he designates as sublime are in fact ideas that throw the mind back toward an awareness of its own indefinite activity. Reflexive consciousness discovers the "shapelessness" of the sublime in its own structure of awareness—a structure unable to "close itself off" with respect to any clear and distinct object of consciousness.[14]

Obviously I cannot insist that this version of the Coleridgean sublime is necessarily the correct one. There is simply not enough evidence upon which to base so firm a conclusion. But I can indicate that this version is at least plausible, and that the relationship between self-consciousness—indeed a version of self-consciousness which could be characterized as an act of apperception—and the experience of the sublime is a relationship that seems to have been recognized by Coleridge.

IV

In his *Notebooks* Coleridge observes, "[let me] think of *myself*—of the thinking Being—the Idea becomes dim whatever it be—so dim that I know not what it is—but the Feeling is deep & steady—and this I call *I*—~~the~~ identifying the Percipient & the Perceived." [15] Coleridge here seems to describe an act of apperception in which the subject intuits the subject *qua* subject. Consciousness, in focusing exclusively upon the self, loses whatever distinct conception it might have had of the self ("the Idea becomes dim"), even to the extent of becoming finally unable to formulate any conception adequate to the intuited reality ("I know not what it is"). But a feeling without a concept remains, and it is this unmediated feeling of self which Coleridge designates as the "*I*." In this feeling, also, there is an identification of "the Percipient & the Perceived." The self as "Perceived," as constituted as an object of reflection, merges into the subjectivity of the "Percipient." Because the idea of self has become "dim," consciousness can no longer constitute itself as a direct object (or as something "Perceived") of thought. The sense of self as object is converted into a sense of self as subject, into a feeling that is "deep & steady."

The question now is to what extent might this structure of reflexive awareness be designated, from a Coleridgean perspective, as "sublime"? In answer we can say, first, that the act of thinking "of the thinking Being" seems to lead to an ideational "dimness" that in certain respects is phenomenologically similar to Coleridge's encounter with the gloom of a Gothic cathedral. There, it will be recalled, Coleridge described himself as feeling as if his "whole being" were expanding "into the infinite." We understood this metaphor of expansion as an expression of a radical alteration in the sense of identity: no longer could the subject define himself in terms of an exclusive spatial identity. Self-awareness developed a sense of the self as having infinitely receded "from shapeliness." Here, in this passage from the *Notebooks*, we find Coleridge describing a similar alteration in the sense of identity: the idea of self, "whatever it be," recedes from whatever "shapeliness" it might have had. The idea of self is rendered obscure and indefinite. Furthermore, just as in the Gothic gloom the subject's sense of its own expansion led to a sense of the fusion of subject and object and a sense of reconciliation between contraries, so here we find the growing obscurity and indefiniteness of the idea of self leading to a fusion of subject and object—in this case the identification of "the Percipient & the Perceived" within a context of introspection. The contraries of self as subject and self as object are resolved, and the "*I*" is completely one with itself by means of a feeling that is "deep & steady." Finally, this passage from the *Notebooks* suggests that insofar as the sense of self becomes, as it were, deconceptualized, the self can no longer introduce a division into the immediate sense of identity by thinking *about* the self by means of a distinct idea of the self. This structure of reflexive awareness is one of which from the point of view of the "*I*" no predication is possible or, if predication be demanded, as one the "*I*" might describe in the sentence "I am nothing!" —here, of course, using the term "nothing" not to deny the existing reality of the "*I*" but to suggest the special nature of that structure of consciousness in which all distinct concepts of the self have disappeared. The self feels itself as "nothing" because it now lacks the means to define itself as any precisely limited "thing."

A second answer to the question of how the act of thinking "of the thinking Being" might be designated, from a Coleridgean perspective, as "sublime" can be developed if we take note of Coleridge's observation that something can be called "sublime in relation to which the exercise of comparison is suspended." [16] Clearly to the extent that consciousness loses all distinct conceptual grasp of its own nature and is reduced to nothing more than a feeling of the "*I*" which is "deep & steady," the possibility of exercising the powers of comparison is reduced. For any act of comparison requires that consciousness be able to direct its attention back and forth between at least two objects of thought. Any such act taking place within a context of introspection in which the "thinking Being" is thinking exclusively about itself, would therefore require consciousness to constitute itself as a direct object of thought in at least two different ways. This act in turn necessarily introduces an element of division into the mind's sense of being one with itself. The exercise of the powers of comparison within a context of introspection in which the "thinking Being" is thinking exclusively about itself, would entail a structure of awareness in which consciousness alternately constitutes itself as a direct object of thought in either *this* way or *that* way. But such an alternation in intentionality is impossible when the "thinking Being" finds its consciousness of self reduced exclusively to a feeling of the *"I"* which is "deep & steady." In this state of awareness the sense of identity precludes any sense of division. The subject is perfectly one with itself *qua* subject and thus cannot, so long as this feeling of the *"I"* is sustained, constitute itself as a direct object of consciousness in at least two different ways (or even in any one way for that matter). Thus the exercise of the mind's powers of comparison is suspended. And this act of apperception can be characterized, from a Coleridgean perspective, as "sublime."

A more significant way of exploring the question of the relationship for Coleridge between self-consciousness and the experience of the sublime opens to us if we look at "Essay XI" from *The Friend*. Here, according to Thorpe, we might find "the clue to the nature . . . of Coleridge's experience of the sublime." [17] In this essay Coleridge asks his readers: "Hast thou ever raised thy mind to the consideration of existence, in and by itself, as the mere act of existing? Hast thou ever said to thyself thoughtfully, It is! heedless in that moment, whether it were a man before thee, or a flower, or a grain of sand,—without reference, in short, to this or that particular mode or form of existence?" [18] Later in the essay Coleridge characterizes this way of regarding reality as an "opening of the inward eye to the glorious vision of that existence which admits of no question out of itself, acknowledges no predicate but the 'I AM IN THAT I AM!'" This "glorious vision" is for Coleridge an "intuition of absolute existence." [19]

If Professor Thorpe is correct, and if Coleridge's account of such an intuition provides us with a clue to the nature of Coleridge's experience of the sublime, we must then ask: what relationship does this very special intuition have to the act of apperception, the act in which, I have been arguing, Coleridge discovers the subjective source of the sublime? Before we can meaningfully face this question, however, we have to consider exactly what Coleridge might mean when he speaks of an "intuition of absolute existence," and exactly how his account of this "glorious vision" might be taken as Thorpe indicates it can be taken.

It would seem that a "consideration of existence" without reference "to this or that particular mode or form of existence" is in fact a way of looking at the universe which prohibits the use of any predicate but the predicate of existence. In this intuition consciousness becomes absolutely "heedless" of the possibility that the universe might be envisaged as a universe composed of *essences*. I use this last term in a Coleridgean sense. He writes in the *Biographia:* "Essence, in its primary signification, means the principle of *individuation,* the inmost principle of the possiblity of any thing, as that particular thing. It is equivalent to the *idea* of a thing." [20] Paradoxically, therefore, all things are especially seen as exhibiting the "mere act of existing" only to the extent that they are *not* seen as individuals. The sense *that* a thing is stands in opposition to the sense of *what* a thing is as this or that particular individual. Consciousness, in forming distinct ideas of individual things, engages in a contemplation of es-

86

sences, of principles of individuation. Only to the extent that it disengages from all such contemplation, only to the extent that it abandons all distinct ideas of individual things, can consciousness move toward an intuition of absolute existence. In short, this "glorious vision" is a vision of existence without essence.

Perhaps all this can be made more clear if we observe that what Coleridge seems to be describing is a structure of consciousness which is directed toward something rather like what certain scholastic theologians would have called "actus purus." For these theologians, of course, the actus purus is none other than God. Gilson points out that Aquinas, for example, conceives of God as nothing more and nothing less than an "absolute act of being"; God is "the being whose whole nature it is to be such an existential act." Therefore, to "say that God 'is this,' or that he 'is that,' would be to restrict his being to the essences of what 'this' and 'that' are. God 'is,' absolutely." [21]

From the point of view of this analogy we might say that Coleridge seems to be suggesting the possibility of a kind of vision for men on earth which most scholastics would have permitted men to obtain only in heaven—a vision that is indeed "beatific" or like the traditional vision of God because, as Coleridge puts it, existence so intuited reveals itself to be "an eternal and infinite self-rejoicing, self-loving, with a joy unfathomable, with a love all-comprehensive." [22] Coleridge's version of the actus purus is not of an absolutely existing being veiled from men's eyes because it exists only in some external otherworld, in some dimension of uncreated reality far removed from the world of time and created being. On the contrary, this act of "existence incomprehensible and groundless" is thoroughly immanent throughout the world of discrete temporal phenomena. It is, according to Coleridge, a "life-ebullient stream which breaks through every momentary embankment, again, indeed, and ever more to embank itself, but within no banks to stagnate or be imprisoned." [23] The vision of absolute existence might be lost at those times when consciousness is directed toward the "momentary embankment" of the *"idea"* or essence of a particular thing, but so powerful and free is absolute existence that these embankments will eventually dissolve. The ideational world of essences will always give way before the intuition of absolute existence.

I believe, along with Professor Thorpe, that in this description of a "glorious vision" of existence Coleridge has presented us with his most valuable, indeed most philosophically precise, account of what constitutes for him the experience of the sublime. We have seen how he postulates that "those objects whose shape most recedes from shapeliness are commonly the exciting occasions" of the experience of the sublime, and we have interpreted this postulate as having reference, not simply to objects possessing a physical shape, but more significantly to certain ideas that, as it were, lose their "shape" by becoming obscure and indistinct. We have also seen that an object contemplated without reference "to this or that particular mode or form of existence" is in fact an object contemplated without reference to its "essence," to the *"idea"* of the thing as that particular thing. From the perspective of the "glorious vision," nothing may be conceived of as an individual thing. To the extent, therefore, that consciousness intuits existence "heedless" of essence, to that same extent does consciousness intuit a world in which all things lose their ideational "shape" as individual things, a world in which all the ideas of individual things must necessarily grow obscure and indistinct. The "consideration of existence, in and by itself" necessitates, in other words, a structure of consciousness absolutely lacking any means whereby any particular thing may be conceived as this or that particular thing. Nor is this absence of a principle of particularization simply a matter of an inability to *conceive* of an individual. Certainly, from the perspective of the "glorious vision," the individual thing may still be contemplated. But precisely because it is contemplated solely under the aspect of existence, and precisely because the existence so revealed is absolute, the individual thing *qua* individual is simply not seen. Thus, everything loses whatever "shape" or distinctness it might have had as an individual; everything becomes an "exciting occasion" of the experience of the sublime. Neither a man nor a flower nor a grain of sand can be either conceived or even seen as an individual. Each is but a "momentary embankment" of the "life-ebullient stream" of absolute existence, and, as consciousness directly intuits this stream, the embankment dissolves away. Both idea and image of the individual "recede from shapeliness."

There are at least two other ways of suggesting that Coleridge's description of this intuition might be taken as an account of what is for him the basic nature of the experience of the sublime. First, we have already observed how according to Coleridge an encounter with the sublime leads to a suspension of the exercise of the comparative powers. It goes almost without saying that "the glorious vision of that existence which admits of no question out of itself" entails a structure of consciousness in which individuals cannot be distinguished one from another, let alone conceived as individuals. But when consciousness cannot make such distinctions, it obviously has been precluded from the possibility of making any comparisons.[24]

Second, we can take note of Coleridge's observation in one of his letters that when the sublime is felt "neither whole nor parts" are seen and distinguished "but unity as boundless or endless allness."[25] Coleridge offers this puzzling formulation in a context where he is attempting to distinguish, among other things, the "grand" and the "majestic" from the sublime. Thus with respect to the "grand," he writes: "When the parts are numerous and impressive, and are predominate, so as to prevent or greatly lessen the attention to the whole, there results the grand." [26] And with respect to the "majestic," he writes: "Where the impression of the whole, i.e., the sense of unity, predominates so as to abstract the mind from the parts—the majestic." [27] We see in these formulations Coleridge's tendency to locate the meaning of aesthetic terms in the subjective effects certain kinds of aesthetic objects have upon the mind of the observer. These formulations thus have phenomenological implications and call attention to the way in which consciousness is directed in the experience of either the sublime or the grand or the majestic. It would seem that the distinction between the grand and the majestic is largely one of emphasis—an emphasis, that is, in the intentionality of the observer. An object, in order to be characterized as either grand or majestic, is presumably "impressive" in some way. But it can be called "grand" only when its "parts are numerous and impressive," and consciousness is thereby directed toward these parts and away from "attention to the whole." And the object can be called "majestic" only when the mind is so caught up in the "impression of the whole" that the parts of the whole tend to recede from consciousness. But in the case of the sublime, consciousness is directed toward neither the parts nor the whole but toward a kind of "unity" that Coleridge cryptically explains as a "boundless or endless allness." Apparently the term "unity" here is not being used in the same way that it is used in the explanation of the majestic, where "the sense of unity" is equated with "the impression of the whole." It seems reasonable to say, therefore, that the "unity" encountered in the experience of the sublime is not to be in any way confused with the "unity" of the whole—obviously it cannot be so taken since in this experience the whole is not even seen. What then is consciousness directed toward when it intends the "unity" of a "boundless or endless allness"? What indeed, with respect to the object deserving the designation "sublime," is the mind attending to when it is attending to neither the whole nor the parts of that object?

Let us understand that the experiencing of a "unity as boundless or endless allness" is the equivalent, in Coleridgean terms, of an "intuition of absolute existence." Obviously this intuition of the "life-ebullient stream" of existence *qua* existence is an intuition of an absolute which is by definition "boundless or endless" and which, precisely because it is nothing but an act of existence or *actus purus,* possesses a perfect "unity." Now with respect to an object, neither the whole nor the parts of which are seen and distinguished, the subject is caught up in a structure of awareness which lacks a principle of individualization, a way of seizing upon any particularized object of awareness. The intended object neither can be particularized with reference to its parts nor can it be apprehended as an individual whole. The phenomenon is "shapeless," obscure and undefined; it imposes no distinct phenomenal limits upon the attention. The intentionality of consciousness is thereby enabled to become "heedless" of the "particular mode or form" it has before it, and can as it were pour through and beyond a form that escapes successful apprehension. In the very escape of this form, both as a whole and with all of its individual parts, consciousness intuits existence without "essence." To put this another way: the open-ended form of, say, a mist-shrouded mountain dislocates consciousness out of a consideration of "essences," a consideration of either the individual whole or the individual parts. The open-ended form becomes, we might almost say, "transparent": a structure of consciousness is now elicited which penetrates through the opacities, the obscuring "momentary embankments," of defined and individuated phenomena. Consciousness now intuits existence as such, the "life-ebullient stream," and this absolute is a "unity of boundless and endless allness."

We now may consider the crucial question: what relationship might this very special intuition have to that kind of self-consciousness I have been calling "apperception"? Insofar as we take Coleridge's account of this intuition as also providing an account of the basic nature of the Coleridgean experience of the sublime, and insofar as we recall that for Coleridge the source of the sublime is to be located in the subject, then we must say that the source of the intuition of absolute existence is also to be located in the subject. Consciousness opens its "inward eye to the glorious vision"; it intuits the act of existence first of all within itself; it intuits its own existent reality without a "principle of individuation," without simultaneously considering itself from the point of view of "essence." Thus we have a structure of consciousness in which the subject cannot constitute itself as an individuated object of thought, a structure of consciousness, in terms borrowed from Wordsworth, "unprofaned" by "form or image" of the self. The subject intuits itself in a way that "acknowledges no predicate but the 'I AM IN THAT I AM!'" Consciousness intuits its own activity without reference "to this or that particular mode or form of existence," and thus intuits its own activity as an absolute. The function of the open-ended form (or, for that matter, the obscure and indistinct idea) in eliciting this state of sublime self-consciousness, is to throw consciousness back upon itself, to make it aware of itself as an indefinitely dynamic agent unable to "close itself off" with respect to any clear and distinct object of consciousness. As the intended object indefinitely escapes from successful apprehension, consciousness becomes immersed in its own indefinitely striving intentionality. Consciousness intuits itself as simply an act, an undefined energy of being, a "boundless or endless allness." Coleridge's metaphor of the "life-ebullient stream" breaking through the "momentary embankments" of discrete phenomena I finally interpret as a metaphor expressive of that structure of consciousness in which the act of apperception, latent in any specific act of perception, suddenly becomes explicit and thus makes it impossible for consciousness to specify its intended object. (Or, in terms again borrowed from Wordsworth, when the light of sense goes out, we see into the life of things—here understanding "life" to refer to that fundamental activity of consciousness that makes possible the entirety of the phenomenal world.) And since the act of apperception is implicit in all acts of perception, an open-ended form in the phenomenal world is not necessarily required to provoke sublime self-consciousness. Even a circle, a perfectly closed form, can become, as we have seen, an "exciting occasion" for the experience of the sublime. And so can "a man . . . or a flower, or a grain of sand." [28]

Coleridge writes in "Essay XI" that if "thou hast mastered this intuition of absolute existence, thou wilt have learnt likewise, that it was this, and no other, which in the earlier ages seized the nobler minds, the elect among men, with a sort of sacred horror. This it was which first caused them to feel within themselves a something ineffably greater than their own individual nature." It was this intuition that raised "them aloft . . . projecting them to an ideal distance from themselves." [29] The phrase "sacred horror" echoes many eighteenth-century commentaries on the sublime, preoccupied as they were with explaining the "delightful horror," the "pleasing terror," the "awful astonishment," and so on, of the experience. And Coleridge's spatial metaphor of the "elect among men" being projected "to an ideal distance from themselves" is perhaps the most subtle version we have seen so far of that habit of eighteenth-century theorists of describing the mind during the experience of the sublime as a kind of expanding space. Of course Coleridge makes it plain that this "distance," to which "nobler minds" are projected, is "ideal," that is, only a "distance" of consciousness. The metaphor is to be taken in the same way that the metaphors of the expanding mind are to be taken in

the earlier commentaries: expressive of a radical alteration in self-consciousness. Those who have been "seized"
by the "intuition of absolute existence" feel within themselves a "something ineffably greater than their own
individual natures." Suddenly the "elect among men"
intuit a reality within themselves which simply cannot
be explained in terms of their sense of themselves as
individuals. In fact, the intuition of absolute existence
stands in total opposition to any ideas they might have
of themselves as individuals. And only to the extent
that all such ideas grow obscure and indistinct, can
they move toward the "glorious vision." The intuition
and the projection of consciousness "to an ideal distance" entails the focusing of awareness into a visionary
sense of "I AM IN THAT I AM!" And from the perspective of this intuition, the individual *as individual* can
only feel "that I am nothing!" as Coleridge himself felt
in the gloom of a Gothic cathedral.

The metaphor, then, of the mind's expansion "into
eternity," as well as the metaphor of the mind's projection "to an ideal distance" from itself, are metaphors
expressive of a visionary act of apperception, in which
consciousness directly intuits its own activity as if it
were the incomprehensible ground of the being of the
entire phenomenal world. No wonder, then, that this
act of sublime self-consciousness is felt with "a sort of
sacred horror."

V

An important conclusion suggested by this analysis is
that for Coleridge the act of apperception can be interpreted as in some way revealing the universe in its
metaphysical depths, as somehow providing contact
with the ultimate principle of reality. And the same is
true, as I have been arguing, for Wordsworth: the
phenomenological similarities between Coleridge's "life-
ebullient stream" and the universally interfused "some-

thing" of "Tintern Abbey" hardly need elaboration at this point. But we must understand that the ultimate principle for both men is the act of consciousness itself, an act that brings into "being" for consciousness the world of perception, for without it that world would simply cease to "exist." Consciousness itself is a kind of creation, and to intuit consciousness in the very quick of its act is to become intimate, however fleetingly, with the one, upholding life of the phenomenal universe.

In a memorable passage from Book II of *The Prelude* Wordsworth describes such a visionary intuition. He claims this intuition was given to him by nature and enabled him to experience a transcendent principle of unity binding the phenomenal world together into an organic whole:

> From Nature and her overflowing soul
> I had receiv'd so much that all my thoughts
> Were steep'd in feeling; I was only then
> Contented when with bliss ineffable
> I felt the sentiment of Being spread
> O'er all that moves, and all that seemeth still,
> O'er all, that, lost beyond the reach of thought
> And human knowledge, to the human eye
> Invisible, yet liveth to the heart,
> O'er all that leaps, and runs, and shouts, and sings,
> Or beats the gladsome air, o'er all that glides
> Beneath the wave, yea, in the wave itself
> And mighty depth of waters. Wonder not
> If such my transports were; for in all things
> I saw one life, and felt that it was joy.
> One song they sang, and it was audible,
> Most audible then when the fleshly ear,
> O'ercome by grosser prelude of that strain,
> Forgot its functions, and slept undisturb'd.[30]

Wordsworth here describes a progressively more intense intuition of the "one life" in "all things." Even though he says that he "saw" this "one life," the passage as a whole makes clear that this intuition is realized in in its purest form when the mind in some way moves beyond the reports of the senses; that this "one life" is really not to be seen at all but can only be somehow "felt" as consciousness moves progressively beyond the phenomenal world. Thus as Wordsworth feels the "sentiment of Being spread / O'er all that moves, and all that seemeth still," there develops a structure of consciousness which is radically open-ended: the feeling of the "sentiment of Being" induces a kind of centrifugal awareness in which consciousness can neither conceptualize its contents ("lost beyond the reach of thought / And human knowledge") nor even locate itself with respect to distinct objects of sight ("to the human eye / Invisible"). And, as Wordsworth makes clear at the end of this passage, this intuition is most vivid (or, characterized as a "song," "Most audible") when the "fleshly ear" no longer reports sounds of the phenomenal world. The song of the "one life" is a spiritual ditty of no tone. We also note that this intuition is characterized in metaphors of fluidity. Wordsworth suggests that it finds its origin in nature and "her overflowing soul." Nature in some way gives him "so much" that "all" his thoughts become "steep'd in feeling," as if to say Wordsworth's own soul begins to overflow with certain feelings that come to dominate his awareness. And the "sentiment of Being" itself is a feeling that somehow spreads, like an overflowing fluid, throughout the phenomenal world.

This passage thus seems to describe an act of apperception in which consciousness comes to a progressively more intense intuition of its own activity as the ground of the phenomenal world. Wordsworth's "sentiment of Being" is, in Coleridgean terms, an intuition of absolute existence; an intuition of the mind's own ubiquitous activity as it constitutes the world of perception. To the extent that the subject becomes progressively aware of its own subjective energy of consciousness, to that same extent is the phenomenal world intuited as possessing a transcendent principle of unity: in this case, that activity of a single mind which enables the phenomenal world to "exist" as an object for a single consciousness. The subject gradually discovers itself as "spread / O'er all that moves, and all that seemeth still." Consciousness intuits itself as interfusing "all that leaps, and runs, and shouts, and sings." Thus "all things" can be seen as exhibiting "one life": for all things indeed possess—and only possess—this unity insofar as the conscious activity that pervades them all is directly intuited by the mind. The fluid "sentiment of Being" can "spread" throughout the phenomenal world in much the same way that Coleridge's "life-ebullient stream" can break through the "momentary embankments" of discrete perceptions: the subject turns inward upon itself; the act of apperception latent in any act of perception begins to grow explicit; a "something" is intuited as universally interfused. The mind begins to intuit a reality that cannot be reported to it by the senses: this reality is indeed "to the human eye / Invisible," and yet it "liveth to the heart." Nor can it be conceptualized; for the direct encounter by the subject with its subjective energies is, by its very nature, "beyond the reach of thought / And human knowledge." And this experience is, as so often in Wordsworth, an encounter with the depths, an exploration of the immanent: for the "sentiment of Being" finally spreads "Beneath the wave, yea, in the wave itself / And mighty depth of waters."

These lines also suggest that for Wordsworth sublime self-consciousness is not necessarily a structure of awareness that abruptly displaces all other kinds of awareness. The "sentiment of Being" here spreads only gradually, progressively. Indeed, it is generally true about Wordsworth's visionary experiences that although there are moments in his poetry when he seems suddenly and totally to be rapt away from the phenomenal world—

97

to be transported, with the light of sense gone out, into "strange seas of Thought, alone"—what is far more usual is a description of a *process* of consciousness which is more or less visionary; a description of a series of acts of perception in which the latent content of apperception is successively more or less explicit. The "fleshly ear" may sleep at times "undisturb'd" and the phenomenal world may sometimes be lost; but a primary ambition of Wordsworth, as I suggested in my analysis of "Tintern Abbey," is to write a poetry celebrating the way in which the visionary mind may discover dwelling-places in nature. The intuition of the "one life" is not to be purchased by the annihilation of the phenomenal world. Rather, this world, or nature, is somehow to be sustained and made to participate in the visionary dimension disclosed in the act of sublime self-consciousness.

In this infinitely delicate task of adjusting his visionary consciousness to nature, Wordsworth's emphasis is thus largely upon mediation, upon marriage. The "sources of sublimity," he writes in "Essay Supplementary to Preface (1815)," are "in the soul of Man"; but poetry, no matter how "ethereal and transcendent," is "yet incapable" of sustaining "her existence without sensuous incarnation." [31] The act of apperception and the act of perception must be adjusted one to the other. For the sake of poetry itself, the centrifugal awareness of feeling the "sentiment of Being" may only be gradual, progressive. And to preserve the possibility both of a true marriage between mind and nature and of the celebration of that marriage in poetry, centrifugal awareness must be balanced against a centripetal awareness that clings to the discrete phenomena of nature, in much the same way the boy of the Fenwick note on the "Immortality Ode" grasped "at a wall or tree to recall" himself from the "abyss of idealism." A visionary mind with ambitions toward poetry cannot overlook the requirement of "sensuous incarnation," and thus must be disciplined in precisely the way Wordsworth claims to have disciplined himself in the "Preface to Lyrical Ballads (1800)": "I have at all times endeavored *to look steadily* at my subject." The visionary poet must attempt to sustain for his consciousness "an atmosphere of sensation in which to move his wings." [32] In short, there must be embankments of the "life-ebullient stream."

Both Wordsworth and Coleridge designate imagination as the power that accomplishes this labor of mediation. We have already seen how imagination, according to Wordsworth, is a power that proceeds from "a sublime consciousness of the soul in her own mighty and almost divine powers." And I have argued that imagination, as it proceeds, enables the mind to sustain and marry its undefined sense of self with the discrete phenomena provided by nature. In Coleridgean terms imagination is the power that mediates between the intuition of absolute existence and the world of essences, of discrete particulars. Or, as Coleridge himself provocatively remarks in the *Notebooks,* "Imagination [is] the laboratory in which Thought elaborates Essence into Existence." [33] That is to say, imagination is the power whereby the world of individual objects— objects that in themselves, in the words of the *Biographia Literaria,* "are essentially fixed and dead" [34]—is re-created into a living and organic whole through involvement with an act of self-consciousness in which the mind directly intuits its own undefined and living energies.

The generic image in Wordsworth's poetry of such a re-created world—a world in which thought is elaborating essence into existence, a world in which imagination is struggling "to idealize and unify" [35] phenomena into a vision of the one life—is the image of nature found in "Tintern Abbey," a nature suggestively disclosing an underworld of open-ended depths in which the poet gradually discovers the organizing ground of being of that phenomenal world: his own consciousness. Imagination interfuses these depths into the surface of nature, and at the same time prevents nature from being swallowed up in them, from being annihilated in the "abyss of idealism." Sublime self-consciousness, though in itself an ineffably blissful experience of transport beyond the phenomenal world, is to be married to that phenomenal world by the power of imagination. And imagination, though proceeding from "a sublime consciousness of the soul in her own mighty and almost divine powers," must, as the creative principle of a poetry of "sensuous incarnation," return to the world of individual objects, the world that, at the same time, sublime self-consciousness progressively attempts to leave behind. Imagination thus tempers the pure freedom of visionary consciousness—a consciousness that in itself strives to be "by form or image unprofaned." The "something" is to be envisioned as ubiquitously interfused throughout the world of perception It is not to be embraced in an act of solipsistic autonomy.

Coleridge was thinking of this crucial labor of mediation, I believe, when he reminded himself in his *Notebooks* to write "to the Recluse that he may insert something concerning *Ego* / its metaphysical Sublimity— & intimate Synthesis with the principle of Coadunation —without *it* every where all things were a waste— nothing." [36] The ego, directly intuited in its "metaphysical Sublimity," is the ultimate source of Wordsworth's vision of the "one life" and the "joy" pervading all things. But this metaphysically sublime ego must at the same time be synthesized with the "principle of Coadunation," with that power of the imagination whereby the mind transforms the phenomenal world into an organic whole. Without this intimate synthesis, the world of discrete objects would remain fixed and dead:

"a waste—nothing." With it, the world becomes a community of living dwelling-places.

VI

The Simplon Pass episode of Book VI of *The Prelude* is perhaps Wordsworth's most complex and dramatic account of imagination's mediation between sublime self-consciousness and the phenomenal world. Just prior to his descent through this apocalyptic landscape, Wordsworth experienced an intensely vivid moment of apperception:

> Imagination—here the Power so called
> Through sad incompetence of human speech,
> That awful Power rose from the mind's abyss
> Like an unfathered vapour that enwraps,
> At once, some lonely traveller.[37]

Wordsworth here describes a moment in which the power of imagination has suddenly erupted into consciousness. We may assume, then, that that act of sublime self-consciousness out of which imagination proceeds has also overtaken the mind. Thus we can understand why, in the lines immediately following, Wordsworth characterizes this moment of imagination's birth as one in which "the light of sense / Goes out, but with a flash that has revealed / The invisible world." [38] Imagination has risen out of the "mind's abyss," those depths of sublime self-awareness in which the subject directly intuits its own transcendent energies. Such an unmediated intuition leads to an abrupt loss of the phenomenal world. It is a moment in which, Wordsworth asserts, "doth greatness make abode" [39]—a moment in which apperception overwhelms perception. To stress the seemingly gratuitous way in which ordinary consciousness is thus snatched away, Wordsworth describes imagination as having come upon him like "an unfathered vapour." Visionary consciousness is suddenly *there*, without apparent reason or justification, and the mind has moved beyond the world of ordinary sensation.

Immediately after this visionary act of apperception, Wordsworth makes his descent through the "narrow chasm" of Simplon Pass. There he comes upon a landscape riddled with opposites:

> The immeasurable height
> Of woods decaying, never to be decayed,
> The stationary blasts of waterfalls,
> And in the narrow rent at every turn
> Winds thwarting winds, bewildered and forlorn,
> The torrents shooting from the clear blue sky,
> The rocks that muttered close upon our ears,
> Black drizzling crags that spake by the way-side
> As if a voice were in them, the sick sight
> And giddy prospect of the raving stream,
> The unfettered clouds and region of the Heavens,
> Tumult and peace, the darkness and the light—
> Were all like workings of one mind, the features
> Of the same face, blossoms upon one tree;
> Characters of the great Apocalypse,
> The types and symbols of Eternity,
> Of first, and last, and midst, and without end.[40]

In this Alpine abyss Wordsworth's imagination discovers a dwelling-place or a "sensuous incarnation" for the visionary thrust of his own sublime self-consciousness—that act elicited in him just prior to his descent. Thus nature's abyss becomes simultaneously a mental abyss: the contradictory phenomena of the chasm appear to be "all like workings of one mind." Indeed, Wordsworth's act of descending is in itself suggestive of that labor of imagination whereby the visionary mind, in which the light of sense has gone out, reestablishes contact with the phenomenal world. Through the mediating energy of imagination, the transcending consciousness at the same time descends from the "invisible world" into the depths of nature, there only to discover itself now made immanent and nature herself becoming symbolic of the "invisible world" of visionary consciousness. The apocalyptic features of Simplon Pass are therefore to be taken as generally expressive of the dialectical relationship that imagination sustains between sublime self-consciousness and the phenomenal world. The discordant phenomena of Simplon Pass are expressive of one mind working in two dialectically opposed directions. On the one hand, they are expressive of the movement of consciousness beyond the phenomenal world. Thus they appear to be "Characters of the great Apocalypse" and "types and symbols of Eternity." On the other hand, they are expressive of imagination's labor of preserving that phenomenal world for consciousness, of infusing the act of apperception into the world of perception: for imagination saves nature in this instance by creating an underworld.

This double direction of consciousness is suggested in complex images of flux and stasis, destruction and preservation, height and depth. The "immeasurable height / Of woods" appears to be "decaying," passing toward that obliteration sublime self-consciousness imposes upon the phenomenal world. Yet at the same time these woods are "never to be decayed"; they are expressive of how imagination sustains nature. Waterfalls plunge downward into the chasm, yet their "blasts" appear to be "stationary," as if to suggest imagination's rescue of the world from an annihilating plunge into the abyss of immanent visionary consciousness. Likewise, "torrents" of winds are "shooting" downward from "the clear blue sky" into the underworld that has been opened up by imagination's infusion of the act of apperception into the world of perception. Yet in the "narrow rent" of the Pass, winds are "thwarting winds," and presumably the destructive movements of these winds and torrents (expressive of the destructive thrust of visionary consciousness) are thereby checked and fixed into a precarious stasis. Nature seems indefinitely suspended in the movement toward apocalypse. Nature hangs over the abyss.[41]

There is a further complexity in the fact that the descending traveler himself feels the threat from that structure of visionary consciousness which he is displacing into nature through the agency of imagination. Rocks mutter close upon his ears, and "Black drizzling crags" speak as "if a voice were in them." The imagery suggests how, to the extent the apocalyptic act of apperception is confined in the world of perception, that world in itself takes on an appearance of being dangerous. The paradox of course is that it is nature that is herself endangered. The descending traveler also feels a threat at "the sick sight / And giddy prospect of the raving stream." The underworld of displaced visionary consciousness opens beneath his feet. Yet Wordsworth maintains his astonishing balance; the dialectical relationship between sublime self-consciousness and the phenomenal world is somehow sustained by imagination. The poet remains poised between the abyss below and the "unfettered clouds and region of the Heavens" above—an emblem of that "invisible world" of pure, transcendent vision from which his consciousness has been descending as it becomes progressively more displaced into nature. And the chasm grows progressively more contradictory as it comes to appear more and more as a mental abyss: the tumult and darkness of a world moving toward destruction are mingled with the peace and light of pure visionary consciousness.

Finally, Wordsworth comes to stand at the very center of an organic universe, the phenomena of which, no matter how contradictory and discordant, are all like "blossoms upon one tree." As Coleridge might put it, the world of essences has been elaborated into an intuition of absolute existence. The dialectical relationship that imagination has sustained permits the poet to see a universe in which the discrete events of nature are inextricably mingled with, and unified in terms of, an intuition of one transcendent mind. All the discordant phenomena of nature exhibit themselves as expressions of a single structure of consciousness, that structure of consciousness in which the subject has an intuition of the activity of his own mind as the ground of being of the phenomenal world—but an intuition that simultaneously poses the ultimate threat to the continued existence of that world. This paradoxical vision is extraordinary: in order that the universe might be seen as an organic whole it must be brought to the very brink of apocalypse. Consciousness by the ego of its own metaphysical sublimity is indeed a consciousness "Of first, and last, and midst, and without end"; a consciousness of, again in Coleridgean terms, a "boundless or endless allness"; an intuition of a dynamic "something" universally interfused. But it is only by the miracle of imagination's triumph that nature can be sustained as symbolic of this intuition and thus transformed. Imagination preserves nature as a "face" expressive of a single transcendent mind.

5

The Syntheses of Imagination

WILLIAM BLAKE once claimed to see in Wordsworth's poetry "the Natural Man rising up against the Spiritual Man Continually," and went on to conclude that Wordsworth is then "No Poet but a Heathen Philosopher at Enmity against true Poetry or Inspiration." [1] In the terms of this essay we might say that what Blake calls Wordsworth's "Natural Man" is the act of perception, an act that posits for the mind the appearance of an extramental universe. Wordsworth's "Spiritual Man" is the act of apperception, an act of visionary self-consciousness which threatens to swallow that phenomenal world into the "abyss of idealism." And what Blake is judging, with characteristic vehemence, is Wordsworth's tendency to allow too much to the appearances, his habit of claiming to find in the "mighty world / Of eye, and ear" what Blake would understand to be solely a projection of the autonomous visionary mind. The rebellion of Wordsworth's "Natural Man" is Wordsworth's habit of interfusing into the phenomenal world what he discovers in the depths of his own self-consciousness, and then claiming that these interfusions are gifts of nature, gifts that are indeed latent in the simplest act of perception. Blake is genuinely perplexed by the discrepancy he sees between Wordsworth's explicit claims for nature and Wordsworth's mental acts as they are manifested in his poetry: "Natural objects always did

& now do weaken, deaden & obliterate Imagination in Me. Wordsworth must know that what he writes Valuable is Not to be found in Nature."[2]

The quarrel between Blake and Wordsworth derives, I suspect, from each poet's different conception of the right use of the imagination. For Blake the principal enemy is the British empirical tradition and all its Lockean works and Newtonian pomps. Thus his imagination is to be used as an organ of strife, of intellectual warfare. The emphasis in his visionary ambition is to bring the "outside" back into the mind, to make clear the radical extent to which the universe of perception is dependent upon the energies of the mind. His imaginative struggle is in many ways an effort toward greater self-consciousness.

For Wordsworth, however, the imagination is to be used for the purposes of love. He will remain, in the words of "Tintern Abbey," "A lover of the meadows and the woods," even at the cost of considerable perplexity—his own as well as Blake's. And he will bestow gifts upon his beloved, even at the cost of surrendering recognition both of what he has given and of what limits his love has placed upon his creative freedom. Thus the emphasis in Wordsworth's visionary ambition is somewhat antivisionary: it is to displace his "inside" outward, to establish an "underconsciousness" beneath the surface of the given phenomenal world. Imagination's task is not to obliterate what Blake suggests has always obliterated imagination in him: the apparent autonomy of the extramental universe. Rather, imagination's task is to cherish that world and to establish a state of mutuality between it and the mind. What Blake sees as a rebellion of Wordsworth's "Natural Man" is quite simply the result of Wordsworth's willingness to accept limits for his "Spiritual Man." It is the result of his desire, out of love, to use his imagination to effect a lasting synthesis between common perception and visionary apperception. The freedom of sublime self-consciousness is to be enjoyed only in a state of fidelity to nature.

This final chapter examines some of the ways of Wordsworth's fidelity. If the act of visionary self-consciousness is to be enjoyed only *sub specie naturae,* then that act must come to terms with the inescapable fact that the external world always appears to be existing within the dimensions of space and time. Thus these questions: What is the form of Wordsworthian space —that very special kind of space which his mind and nature come simultaneously to inhabit through the mediating power of imagination? And what is the form of Wordsworthian time? How is the temporal reality of the phenomenal world transformed by the act of imagination?

Another inescapable fact of the external world is that it is filled with things that are often ignored and, in the words of Shelley, obscured behind the "film of familiarity." A poet like Wordsworth who chooses to be a lover of that mighty world of eye and ear, and who pledges to be as faithful as possible to "the life / In common things—the endless store of things," [3] such a poet can make no discriminations in his love. Indeed, he has a special obligation to cherish what is usually ignored, what seems insignificant, even trivial in that endless store. Wordsworth himself recognized this obligation in declaring that his poetic task is to make the humble sublime. And thus my final question is: What is the relationship between Wordsworth's explicitly formulated program and the structure of his imaginative act?

No attempt is made in this concluding chapter to exhaust the answers to these enormously complicated questions. Instead, I choose to move on a high level of provocative generality, and nowhere insist that these questions, once they have been caught in the light of my analysis of the structure of Wordsworth's imaginative act, have been in any final way "answered." What follows, then, is offered as nothing more than a set of deliberately brief sketches, a drawing out from my thesis of some sets of coordinates which may help other readers of Wordsworth to achieve a critical purchase upon a specific problem in a specific poem.

II

What is the form of Wordsworthian space?

The poet asserts that in "nature everything is distinct, yet nothing defined into absolute independent singleness."[4] The space occupied by any individual phenomenon is likewise not an absolutely closed space. Though things may be distinctly located in space, they cannot claim exclusive possession of their location. As Alfred North Whitehead observes in his *Science and the Modern World*, Wordsworth's "theme is nature *in solido*, that is to say, he dwells on that mysterious presence of surrounding things, which imposes itself on any separate element that we set up as an individual for its own sake. He always grasps the whole of nature as involved in the tonality of the particular instance."[5] It is of course the power of imagination that creates this oxymoronic "tonality," this sense of an individual phenomenon as somehow having "involved" in itself, or rolled up into itself (L. *involvere*, to roll into), or contained within itself the whole of nature. For imagination is the faculty, according to Wordsworth, whereby "things are lost in each other, and limits vanish."[6] Not only do phenomena in themselves tend to become intermingled, their presences interfusing with one another, but their spatial "limits" as well tend to be obliterated. The individual form comes no longer to be seen as a "punctual Presence,"[7] existing at a defined point in space that excludes all other points in space. Rather, the place of any one thing exhibits the potential of including all other places.[8] The locations of Wordsworthian space are thus somewhat deceptive: though they are special places seemingly isolated from the rest of the world, they can also be, at the same time and in a certain way, so interfused with the presence of all surrounding things that these special places tend to be radically open-ended, indeed sometimes functioning almost like a point of view, rather than a point of space, through which the mind might pass toward a vision of the totality of things. The places of Wordsworthian space are thus capable of being transformed by imagination into a series of mutually immanent locations, each of which simultaneously contains and is contained by the other. "Surrounding things" are at the same time "involved" or rolled up into the "tonality of the particular instance"; they can in some way be both around and within.

An example of such a peculiarly immanent place or location is the hill-enclosed lake in the vale of Grasmere:

> Behold the universal imagery
> Inverted, all its sun-bright features touched
> As with the varnish, and the gloss of dreams;
> Dreamlike the blending also of the whole
> Harmonious landscape; all along the shore
> The boundary lost, the line invisible
> That parts the image from reality;
> And the clear hills, as high as they ascend
> Heavenward, so piercing deep the lake below.[9]

Wordsworth's imperative "Behold" directs the eye toward a single phenomenon, the lake of Grasmere. But we immediately discover that contained in the lake is "the universal imagery / Inverted." The "clear hills" surrounding the lake are simultaneously immanent within the lake, and in that state of immanence assume a suggestively visionary appearance: they seem to be "touched" with the "varnish, and the gloss of dreams." We cannot assume that this appearance of "varnish" and "gloss" is merely the result of the phenomenal difference between the hills when seen directly and the hills when seen "Inverted" or reflected upon the surface of the lake. For, as Wordsworth tells us, the "line" that "parts the image from reality" is "invisible," not only indicating the invisibility of the lake's shoreline but also suggesting the difficulty of making phenomenal distinctions between the hills in themselves and their reflected image. The hills, at the same time ascending into the sky and "piercing deep" into the lake, are seen in both actions as "clear Hills." Is it, then, simply this "blending" of image and reality—simultaneously a doubling of appearances—which accounts for Wordsworth's assertion that the overall impression is "Dreamlike"?

A better reason for Wordsworth's characterization can be given if we recall that for the poet the act of imagination fuses that open-ended sense of self experienced in the act of apperception with the phenomena of nature revealed by the act of perception. Here in the lake of Grasmere, Wordsworth beholds almost a paradigm of that oxymoronic fusion—an emblem of imaginative consciousness. We notice that the lake, through its reflection of the hills that "ascend Heavenward," is endowed with an open-ended space, for the hills also appear to be "piercing" heavenward into its depths. Not only is the lake indistinguishable along its shoreline from the surrounding and ascending landscape but also inwardly dilated and deepened by its reflection of that ascending landscape. Thus the lake takes on the appearance of a potentially infinite expansion in all directions. It is precisely in this expansion that the lake becomes suggestively emblematic. Just as in the experience of imaginative consciousness the spatial limits of the self are felt to be dissolving, so the spatial limits of the lake appear to be dissolving. Yet also here, as for imaginative consciousness, the phenomenal world is not lost. The blending of the "whole

/ Harmonious landscape" into an open-ended focus does not lead to an apocalyptic confusion or destruction of that landscape. Though the "universal imagery" may be "inverted" in a lake that appears to be bottomless, that "imagery" is not obliterated in that space: the hills remain "clear." Thus, taking this scene as emblematic, we might say that the phenomenal world has been tranquilly married to the "abyss of idealism." The sense of the infinite is quietly discovered to be immanent in the sense of the finite.

All this generally suggests that the mutual immanence of the special locations in Wordsworth's landscape are to be taken as expressive of the ubiquitous energy of consciousness interfused by the power of imagination throughout the phenomenal world. No single location can be "defined into absolute independent singleness" because each location, as an object of perception, is potentially exposed to the dilating power of the act of apperception. Imagination, Wordsworth observes, deals "with objects not as they are, but as they appear to the mind of the poet." [10] The places in Wordsworth's landscape are thus dependent for their poetic appearance upon a mind that is capable of acts of sublime self-consciousness, acts in which all limits, spatial or otherwise, are felt to be vanishing. All places have the potential for mutual immanence to the extent that the "sentiment of Being" spreads through phenomenal space. The mind's perception of any specific location can be transformed into an experience of the mind's simultaneously moving beyond that location insofar as the act of apperception, the Coleridgean "I AM IN THAT I AM" latent in any act of perception, becomes explicit. For in this structure of self-consciousness, when experienced in its purest form, the mind feels itself to be confined to no particular place. Also, the oxymoronic appearance of the "particular instance," into which according to Whitehead the whole of nature has been somehow "involved," is expressive of imagination's gathering into a single focus in phenomenal space of that ubiquitous activity of consciousness that, as we saw in "Tintern Abbey," "rolls through all things." When the sense of unlocalized self is fused, through imagination, with a location in the phenomenal world, that fixed location begins to take on the appearance of being filled, in some barely describable way, with other locations.

According to the Wanderer of *The Excursion,* there is an *"active* Principle" that "subsists / In all things." This "Spirit" is one that

> knows no insulated spot,
> No chasm, no solitude; from link to link
> It circulates, the Soul of all the world.
> This is the freedom of the universe.[11]

The mind, in moving toward an intuition of this "Spirit," achieves a sense of its own spatial "freedom" as well as of the spatial "freedom" of the phenomenal universe in which there comes to appear "no insulated spot." Wordsworth reinterprets the principle of the continuity of the Great Chain of Being into a principle of immanence: a single ubiquitous "Soul" strangely "circulates" through the links of the Chain. The *"active* Principle" disclosed in sublime self-consciousness is the force that breaks down all limits and tends to destroy all sense of isolated points in space. The "freedom of the universe" depends upon the power of consciousness to escape the tyranny of feeling itself confined to a "punctual Presence." And Wordsworth's preoccupation with special places in the landscape, a preoccupation that Hartman refers to as the "spot-syndrome" and traces through the poetry of Wordsworth's major period, is, in the terms of this essay, a preoccupation with the immanence of apperception in perception, an immanence that can be brought to a peculiarly visionary focus in phenomenal space by the power of imagination.[12] There are indeed "Souls of lonely places." [13]

What is the form of Wordsworthian time?

The question is closely related to one of Wordsworth's major themes: the problem of human hope. The despondent Solitary in Book III of *The Excursion* raises the problem in "bitter language of the heart":

> what good is given to men,
> More solid than the gilded clouds of heaven?
> What joy more lasting than a vernal flower?—
> . . . .
> Oh! tremble, ye, to whom hath been assigned
> A course of days composing happy months,
> And they as happy years; the present still
> So like the past, and both so firm a pledge
> Of a congenial future, that the wheels
> Of pleasure move without the aid of hope:
> For Mutability is Nature's bane;
> And slighted Hope *will* be avenged; and, when
> Ye need her favours, ye shall find her not;
> But in her stead—fear—doubt—and agony! [14]

The Solitary's words are interesting, not because of the traditional complaint about nature's mutability which they echo but because of the special warning he directs toward those who live a life of "happy years" in which the present is "So like the past" that both seem to "pledge" an equally happy or "congenial future." In such a state there appears to be a virtual identity between past, present, and future; indeed, such a state might almost be called changeless or timeless. The virtue of hope, irrelevant in a world that is felt to be pleasantly changeless, is therefore never practiced. And

114

when the inevitable reality of destructive change erupts into such a world—as it did for the Solitary—hope, the virtue that was slighted because there seemed no need for it, will be found lacking. The experience of human changelessness is thus both dangerous and ironic. The fact is that the "good . . . given to men" is only as substantial as the fool's gold of the "gilded clouds of heaven"; and if we experience too many identical days in which "the wheels / Of pleasure move without the aid of hope," we will fall into despair when mutability intrudes with its baneful reality. To live without hope, even when appearances seem to permit such a life, is to prepare oneself for the "agony" of hopelessness.

The Wanderer, in one of his many attempts in the poem to "correct" the Solitary's despondency, projects a vision in Book IV

> Of Life continuous, Being unimpaired;
> That hath been, is, and where it was and is
> There shall endure,—existence unexposed
> To the blind walk of mortal accident;
> From diminution safe and weakening age;
> While man grows old, and dwindles, and decays;
> And countless generations of mankind
> Depart; and leave no vestige where they trod.[15]

The Wanderer does not urge hope upon the Solitary by denying the reality of change. For that would be to urge the same trap that the Solitary had already warned against, and into which he had fallen. Hope cannot be purchased by a refusal to face mutability. Indeed, the Wanderer stresses the sad facts of the "blind walk of mortal accident." Man not only stumbles blindly ahead in time, not knowing what "accidents" of violent change he will encounter in his journey, but he also is "blind" to those who have lived before him: decay and death so absolutely overtake "countless generations" of *homines viatores* that "no vestige" of their human existence is

115

left "where they trod." Time and change, it would seem, enforce upon man a sense of irremedial discontinuities.

In the case of the Solitary it was a number of experiences of such discontinuities—of violent snappings of the expectations that had bound him hopefully to the future—which occasioned his despair. How, then, is the Wanderer advocating hope in these lines? By suggesting that there is available to man a vision of an "existence unexposed" to mutability, a vision that transcends the blindness of the "walk of mortal accident." This vision is not of a frozen eternity standing outside the temporal world, nor even of a state of timelessness to be somehow achieved within this world. It is rather of a dimension of reality where "Life" is "continuous" and "Being" remains "unimpaired." In this dimension there is a past, a present, and a future. And "Being" presumably appears to "become" in the sense that it is seen as moving from a past through a present and into a future. But this movement is characterized by a continuous endurance of what "Being" essentially is as it moves through time: "That hath been, is, and, where it was and is / There shall endure." The Wanderer seems to be suggesting, then, that hope is possible in an apprehension of a "becoming," a movement ahead through time, which in some mysterious way is distinguishable from, indeed "unexposed" to, change. The feeling of destructive discontinuity which occasions despair can be resisted if man somehow can come to feel the flow of time as no longer exclusively producing the "bane" of mutability. Within the very flow of time itself, upon the surface of which is scattered undeniable evidence of man's "diminution" and "weakening," there can be intuited, in Wordsworth's words, "the great moving spirit of things." [16] Hope is to be rooted in the enduring heart of the temporal process—in a vision of a duration that subsists beneath all discontinuities.

How is this saving vision to be achieved? We recall from chapter 3 of this essay how the Wanderer (there discussed under his other name in the poem, the Pedlar) was "endowed" by an early and prolonged exposure to the sublime forms of nature with the "vision and the faculty divine"; that is, with the power of sublime self-consciousness.[17] We might say, then, that his vision of a duration that subsists beneath all discontinuities—a vision that is also Wordsworth's—is the result of imagination's infusing the perceived world of mutability with that sense of time experienced in the act of apperception. This structure of awareness not only releases consciousness from the sense of being confined to a particular location in space, it also releases consciousness from the sense of being confined to a particular moment in time. The subject in directly intuiting itself achieves a structure of consciousness that absolutely lacks any principle of limitation—any means, with respect to time, whereby the self might define itself as existing exclusively at this particular moment. The sense of the self's expansion outward into space is paralleled and accompanied by a sense of the self's "expansion" backward and forward in time. Consciousness feels itself, therefore, not only interfusing all space but also interfusing all time. As Wordsworth observes in *The Prelude,* after having recalled the particularly visionary quality of his first encounter with London:

> Such is the strength and glory of our Youth.
> The Human nature unto which I felt
> That I belong'd, and which I lov'd and reverenc'd,
> Was not a punctual Presence, but a Spirit
> Living in time and space, and far diffus'd.
> In this my joy, in this my dignity
> Consisted.[18]

Sublime self-consciousness evokes a sense of a self that is "far diffus'd" throughout time as well as space. In both dimensions consciousness feels itself to be much more than a "punctual Presence."

117

We might thus say that the perceived moment of the world of mutability, once it has been invaded by the act of apperception through the mediation of imagination, becomes an immanent moment. It now appears to be filled with both past and future. The sense of the self's diffusion throughout time is displaced or focused by imagination into the phenomenal moment and redeems it, as it were, from being merely an exclusive instant in the world of mutability, that world of absolute and frequently violent discontinuities. Such an exclusive instant would in itself appear to be absolutely discontinuous, severed from past instants and future instants, resembling nothing more than a mathematical point without extension. A succession of such mutually exclusive instants constitutes the time in which despair flourishes. But the moment invaded by sublime self-consciousness appears at the same time to be invaded by moments of the past and moments of the future. There is thus possible a vision of a continuous duration "whose heterogeneous moments," in the words of Bergson, "permeate one another." [19] This is the characteristic intuition of a man who leads, in Wordsworth's terms, a "life where hope and memory are as one." [20] All of which is to say that hope is a function of an intuition of an essentially continuous flow of time within the often fragmented time of the world of mutability. Imagination, by projecting into this fragmented time a sense of the self's simultaneous existence at all moments of time, endows the temporal process with the appearance of possessing a continuous duration. Consciousness is now enabled, in the words of Poulet, "to travel through time in order to feel its continuity." It is in this feeling —what Poulet might call the "romanticism of *experienced continuity*"—that hope resides.[21] The heart, having overcome the oppressive sense of time's irremedial discontinuities, can now begin to hope. It can project its desire into a seemingly limitless future. No wonder, then, that Wordsworth's remembering in Book

VI of *The Prelude* of his Alpine encounter with imagination's power causes him to feel a "hope that can never die." [22]

We can now consider the function of memory in Wordsworth's poetic process. According to the well-known formulation of the "Preface to the Lyrical Ballads (1800)," poetry "is the spontaneous overflow of powerful feelings: it takes its origin from emotion recollected in tranquillity: the emotion is contemplated till, by a species of reaction, the tranquillity gradually disappears, and an emotion, kindred to that which was before the subject of contemplation, is gradually produced, and does itself actually exist in the mind." [23] How are we to reconcile the thesis of this essay, that Wordsworth's act of imagination proceeds from an act of apperception, with Wordsworth's assertion here that poetry "takes its origin from emotion recollected in tranquillity"? Can we say that the "spontaneous overflow"—which appears to be the result of a "species of reaction" by the mind to its originally tranquil and contemplative memory of an emotion—is likewise the result of an act of apperception? The answers to these questions obviously depend on our interpretation of this "species of reaction." What is this *kind* of reaction by consciousness to its own activity which according to Wordsworth triggers the "overflow" of emotion into poetic form?

Let us first notice that the metaphor of "overflow," one of the constituting metaphors of Wordsworth's expressive theory of art, is suggestive, when taken merely as an image and not as a metaphor, of an act of *spreading* or *diffusion* of some liquid substance in space. We can next recall how the song of the Solitary Reaper, producing in Wordsworth an intense imaginative reaction, is described as "overflowing" the "Vale profound" in which the harvesting girl is seen.[24] In this image of a spatialized sound, a sound that spreads and expands like a growing body of water, there is to be detected, I believe, another expression of that spreading and expansion so characteristic of sublime self-consciousness. Can we also detect in Wordsworth's metaphor of the "overflow of powerful feelings" an echo of the act of apperception? Are we permitted to say that the metaphor is but another version of those metaphors of apperception we have already seen: of a self "far diffus'd" in time and space; of the "sentiment of Being" spreading throughout the phenomenal world?

We should also notice that these "powerful feelings" that "overflow" are "kindred to that which was before the subject of contemplation," that is, they resemble the original "emotion recollected in tranquillity." It might be said, then, the contemplative act that leads to poetry also leads to a "re-feeling" of a past emotion. Can we not further say, therefore, that Wordsworth's contemplative act brings back a feeling from the past into present consciousness, and in this respect the psychological genesis of poetry for Wordsworth is an act of consciousness in which the mind overcomes any sense it might have of feeling itself confined to the emotions of the present? The emotions of the past can be made to rise up again in present consciousness. And in this experience—what we would now call the act of "affective memory"—consciousness discovers itself no longer confined to an emotive "punctual Presence." The invasion of the present by feelings from the past seems to provoke a sense of the self as "far diffus'd" in time. The "powerful feelings" that "overflow" into poetry proceed from a "far diffus'd" subjectivity that has discovered, through affective memory, its ability to transcend its location in the present. Apperceiving consciousness in turn powerfully "spreads" itself into poetry. Just as such a structure of awareness becomes interfused throughout the phenomenal world, so language becomes, in Wordsworth's terms, "an incarnation of the thought." [25]

I cannot insist upon the inescapable correctness of

this interpretation both of Wordsworth's unexplained "species of reaction" and of the key metaphor in his formulation of an expressive theory of art. The language of Wordsworth's description of the psychological origins of poetry is finally more provocative than definitively and precisely illuminating. But the power of the affective memory to induce an act of sublime self-consciousness is clearly suggested in a passage from Book II of *The Prelude* where, recalling how as a child he would wander through nights "blackened with a coming storm," Wordsworth observes:

> Thence did I drink the visionary power;
> And deem not profitless those fleeting moods
> Of shadowy exultation: not for this,
> That they are kindred to our purer mind
> And intellectual life; but that the soul,
> Remembering how she felt, but what she felt
> Remembering not, retains an obscure sense
> Of possible sublimity, whereto
> With growing faculties she doth aspire,
> With faculties still growing, feeling still
> That whatsoever point they gain, they yet
> Have something to pursue.[26]

The value Wordsworth finds in memories of certain "fleeting moods / Of shadowy exultation" is that they enable the "soul" to retain "an obscure sense / Of possible sublimity." This introspective and potentially visionary traffic with the past—and here Wordsworth makes a curious distinction—depends upon the soul's remembering, not "what she felt," but "how she felt." The special concern of this act of memory seems to be not so much with the exact content of a certain past feeling, but with what we might almost call the "feeling" of that past feeling—a "feeling" detached from any of the specific circumstances of the past surrounding the original feeling. What is to be recovered from the past is a "how," a mode of pure subjectivity, not a "what," a subjectivity defined with respect to any specific past object of consciousness. The feeling is to be refelt, not to be recalled.[27] The feeling is to be dislodged from its location in a remembered past and therefore permitted to be refelt in the present. The labor of memory that accomplishes this recovery is in itself an open-ended activity: there always remains "something" of the subjectivity of the past "to pursue." This pursuit also and significantly induces a form of self-consciousness in which the soul feels its "faculties" or powers to be "growing" in a similarly open-ended fashion: the subject intuits itself in such a way that its powers seem to be potentially infinite. The language of Wordsworth's account of this act of affective memory subtly weaves together both a description of an infinite regression by consciousness into its past subjectivity and a description of a simultaneously intensifying act of self-consciousness in which the soul comes to a progressively incremental sense of its own powers. Indeed, Wordsworth's loose and open syntax, permitting him to pass almost unnoticeably from a discussion of an act of memory into a discussion of an act of self-consciousness, finally suggests that both acts are in essence identical. The "point" that the powers of the soul may "gain" can be taken to refer both to a stage in the retrospective apprehension of a past mode of subjectivity and to a stage in the intensification of self-consciousness. And for both acts there remains a "something" to be pursued, a provocative "something" that is latent—or can we say interfused?—in the mind's "obscure sense / Of possible sublimity." It would seem that for Wordsworth one of the principal means for inducing sublime self-consciousness is the act of affective memory.

Thus it should not be surprising that Wordsworth uses metaphors of depth and of immanence to describe the act of memory. In one of the more elaborate similes

of *The Prelude,* Wordsworth characterizes the activity
of his mind in writing that autobiographical poem:

> As one who hangs down-bending from the side
> Of a slow-moving boat, upon the breast
> Of a still water, solacing himself
> With such discoveries as his eye can make
> Beneath him in the bottom of the deep,
> Sees many beauteous sights—weeds, fishes, flowers,
> Grots, pebbles, roots of trees, and fancies more,
> Yet often is perplexed and cannot part
> The shadow from the substance, rocks and sky,
> Mountains and clouds, reflected in the depth
> Of the clear flood, from things which there abide
> In their true dwelling; now is crossed by gleam
> Of his own image, by a sun-beam now,
> And wavering motions sent he know not whence,
> Impediments that make his task more sweet;
> Such pleasant office have we long pursued
> Incumbent o'er the surface of past time.[28]

The act of memory is here compared to an exploration
of an immanent space—a comparison produced by
Wordsworth's spatialization of time: "past time" has a
"surface." Thus the act of looking *backward* into time
is analogous to the act of looking *downward* into space.
Just as in "Tintern Abbey" Wordsworth's memory play-
ing over the surface of the landscape gradually brings
his consciousness *down into* the heart of the landscape,
there to postulate the presence of an unseen hermit, so
here memory is depicted as a search for "such dis-
coveries" as can be made in the "bottom of the deep."
But what is discovered in the "deep" of this simile is
not a direct vision into the "life of things" but a world
remarkably like the world created by the power of
imagination, one of whose functions, we have already
observed, is to produce a state of appearances in which

"things are lost in each other, and limits vanish." Here, in the depths of this "still water" of time, "shadow" cannot be parted from "substance"; and the "rocks and sky, / Mountains and clouds" cannot be distinguished "from things which there abide / In their true dwelling." In other words, images from the present are confused with images from the past. The suggestion is that Wordsworth's act of memory elicits in him the power of imagination, the power that presumably enables him to write *The Prelude* and in this simile is implicitly described as mingling perceptions from the past with perceptions from the present. But if imagination is stirred by memory, then memory must also in some way provoke that act of sublime self-consciousness out of which imagination proceeds. Here imagination's mingling of past and present within the "deep" of retrospection might be taken as an expression of the implicit presence of that structure of consciousness which knows no location in time. And the simile as a whole suggestively projects an image of the extraordinarily complex relationship in Wordsworth's psychology of creation between the act of memory, the act of imagination, and the latent act of apperception that collapses hard and fast distinctions between past and present.

Perhaps nowhere in Wordsworth is the power of memory to elicit imaginative consciousness more clearly recognized than in his comments on the "spots of time." These "locations" in the past—again Wordsworth spatializes his sense of time—are special memories to which he explicitly repairs for the purpose of inducing in himself a certain state of self-consciousness: a sense that the mind is "lord and master" of the phenomenal world, and "that outward sense / Is but the obedient servant of her will." [29] But is not such a state of self-consciousness exactly that required for the activity of imagination as it "dissolves, diffuses, and dissipates, in order to recreate" the world into art? [30] Thus we might say that the "spots of time" are certain remembered perceptions in which there is a latent content of apperception, a content that is recoverable by the affective memory. These locations in the past are the "hiding-places of man's power"—mysteriously immanent places in which there lurks the presence of visionary consciousness. The mind, in repairing to these "spots of time," seeks a "vivifying Virtue," the power ultimately of transforming the universe into a vision of vital wholeness.[31] The mind seeks for itself a sense of "how" it felt rather than a sense of "what" it felt. It pursues an explication of that "obscure sense / Of possible sublimity" buried in certain haunting images from the past.

One such "spot of time" in *The Prelude* is the famous boating episode of Book I. Wordsworth recalls how after his terrifying vision of a "huge peak" uprearing "its head" above the "horizon's bound," a vision of a "grim shape" which seemed to stride after him "with purpose of its own," there ensued a period of "many days" in which his mind

> Worked with a dim and undetermined sense
> Of unknown modes of being; o'er my thoughts
> There hung a darkness, call it solitude
> Or blank desertion. No familiar shapes
> Remained, no pleasant images of trees,
> Of sea or sky, no colours of green fields;
> But huge and mighty forms, that do not live
> Like living men, moved slowly through the mind
> By day, and were a trouble to my dreams.[32]

This encounter with an almost numinous presence, suddenly and provocatively rising up out of the depths of the phenomenal world, seems to have provoked a sustained act of apperception in which there was a total loss, or apocalypse, of the phenomenal world: "No familiar shapes / Remained." Subjectivity was thrown back upon itself in an intuition of "unknown modes of being." The intuition itself is characterized as a "dim and undetermined sense"; that is, consciousness was unable to define its intentionality with respect to any precisely intended object. In Coleridgean terms, the "shapeless" had overwhelmed the "shapely." For Wordsworth this sustained condition of apperception was a "solitude / Or blank desertion." And his language gropes incrementally through a series of negations to express that same structure of consciousness which in "Tintern Abbey" he attempts to define through the use of the metaphor of dwelling-places.

But most significant about this "spot of time," haunting as it is in itself, is the "species" of Wordsworth's reaction to his remembering of this episode within the context of that unfolding act of memory which is *The Prelude*. For immediately after his recounting of this episode, we find the poet reacting—as he does frequently in the poem—to what his memory has just brought forth. Here, suggestively enough, he breaks out into an apostrophe to the

> Wisdom and Spirit of the universe!
> Thou Soul that art the eternity of thought,
> That givest to forms and images a breath
> And everlasting motion.[33]

These lines suggest an abrupt recovery, through an act of affective memory, of the content of apperception latent in the remembered perceptions of the boating episode. Suddenly Wordsworth addresses a "Soul" that is both an "eternity of thought" and a power that endows the "forms and images" of the phenomenal world with a "breath." The act of apperception both induces a sense of the self's presence throughout all time and almost desubstantializes nature, endowing it through the agency of imagination with the appearance of "Spirit" (L. *spiritus*, breath).

The boating episode of *The Prelude*, then, when read in conjunction with Wordsworth's immediately succeeding apostrophe, can be taken as a significant gloss upon the theory of the psychological origins of poetry set forth in the "Preface to the Lyrical Ballads." The highest function of recollection for Wordsworth is to induce a state of sublime self-consciousness out of which the creative activity of imagination might proceed. Memory is the means whereby the poet might recover a vivifying sense of his identity as a poet, a means of returning through the past to his visionary possibilities in the present. Wordsworth concludes his apostrophe with testimony of a renewed recognition of the "grandeur in the beatings of the heart." [34] The sense of possible sublimity has been transformed into a sense of actual sublimity.

And, as we have seen, it is precisely in this transformation of self-consciousness that hope resides. The intuition of a "grandeur" in the depths of one's subjectivity is also potentially an intuition of a continuous duration in the phenomenal world—a vision of a presence eternally interfused by imagination throughout the images of despair, the bleak evidences of discontinuity, which are strewn across the surface of time. Hence one of Wordsworth's most persistent and poignant fears is that the passing of time will introduce an irremedial break between his present consciousness and those memories that contain "power," those "spots of time" out of which he can educe a sense of himself as "far diffus'd" throughout all of time.

But he fights against this fear by conceiving of poetry as a means of insuring the possibility of continuing hope. The poet writes, according to the "Preface to the Lyrical Ballads," out of a "deep impression of certain inherent and indestructible qualities of the human mind." [35] The eternity of consciousness is somehow to be given "incarnation" in the language of poetry, and poems themselves can thereby become dwelling-places for the "something" that knows no fixed location in time. To the extent that they become such embodiments of sublime self-consciousness, they serve the end of "future restoration." Affective memory, Wordsworth discovers, is not sufficiently reliable, and language is to be summoned to its aid:

> The days gone by
> Come back upon me from the dawn almost
> Of life: the hiding-places of my power
> Seem open; I approach, and then they close;
> I see by glimpses now; when age comes on,
> May scarcely see at all, and I would give,
> While yet we may, as far as words can give,
> A substance and a life to what I feel:
> I would enshrine the spirit of the past
> For future restoration.[36]

The writing of poetry is for Wordsworth a human strategy designed to overcome both the sense of temporal discontinuity and ultimately the sense of despair that such discontinuity provokes. If affective memory is someday to fail—here Wordsworth suggests how his very "approach" to the immanent spaces of the past causes them paradoxically to "close"—then perhaps the content of apperception latent in the perceptions of the past can somehow be enshrined in language for the end of "future restoration." [37] Thus to write poetry is for Wordsworth to cultivate a "life where hope and memory are as one." It is also to cultivate the possibility of future poetry. And it is finally to make an implicit confession of the genuine danger that his sense of self may someday be confined to a "punctual Presence," and that the expectations that bind him hopefully to both past and future may be broken in an irretrievable loss of the power of visionary apperception.

IV

What is the relationship between the structure of Wordsworth's imaginative act and his explicitly formulated poetic program?

If in the "lonely places" of nature there can be detected "Souls" that permit the mind to transcend the isolation of these places, and if at any single moment in time there can be experienced a sense of the self's diffusion throughout all moments in time, then it should not be surprising that even in the "meanest flower that blows" there can be discovered thoughts that "lie too deep for tears." The visionary act of apperception not only can alter dramatically Wordsworth's sense of time and space but also can invade and transform *any* phenomenon, even the most insignificant, into a source of possible sublimity. Thus the poet is entitled to discover visionary possibilities in whatever he chooses to look at, even in a lowly daffodil. As imagination fuses sublime self-consciousness with the "meanest flower that blows," that flower begins to take on an appearance of immanence and thereby can begin to serve as a source of thoughts that "lie too *deep* for tears." [38] The finite and mortal world can be made to reveal a dimension of reality in which the "tears" produced by the mortality of things are made irrelevant. Sublime self-consciousness, a structure of awareness that lacks any principle of limitation, an intuition of "existence" without any principle of "essence"—this act of self-consciousness induces in the subject a sense of itself as an "eternity of thought." The idea of the possible death of the subject is thereby absolutely excluded.[39] And when this sense of self is projected by imagination into the phenomenal world, even the mortality of that world appears to have been somehow overcome. The "noisy years" come to seem but "moments in the being / Of the eternal Silence." [40] And any phenomenon within those "noisy years," even the humblest flower blossoming toward its own extinction, can become mysteriously suggestive of the "eternal Silence" discoverable in the depths of subjectivity.

That a single phenomenon can serve as an oxymoronic emblem of mortality and immortality is an expression of what Meyer Abrams has called the "central paradox" lurking "in the oracular passages of Wordsworth's major period: the oxymoron of the humblegrand, the lofty-mean, the trivial-sublime." [41] This paradox is also implicit in both Wordsworth's descriptions of the poetic mind and his own formulations of his mission as a poet. In the "Essay Supplementary to the Preface (1815)," he discusses the difficulty some readers might have in appreciating his poetry, and observes that "if we consider . . . how remote is the practice and the course of life from the sources of sublimity, in the soul of Man, can it be wondered that there is little existing preparation for a poet charged with a new mission to extend its kingdom, and to augment and spread its enjoyments." [42]

In the words "extend" and "spread" we see still another echo of those metaphors used to describe sublime self-consciousness: the sense of sublimity encountered by the poet in his own soul is to be "spread" through the language of poetry into the minds of his readers. But first of all the poet, whose mission is "to extend the kingdom" of the sublime, must interfuse his own visionary self-consciousness with areas of experience where previously there was not even an obscure sense of possible sublimity. The poem thus becomes the expression, the verbal image of this paradoxical transformation of the phenomenal world. And as such it can serve as a hiding-place of the power whereby the reader himself can begin to discover possible sublimity where once none was thought to exist, but only on the condition that he does not pursue a "practice" and a "course of life" that makes it impossible for him to recover the "sources of sublimity" in his own soul. The ideal reader of Wordsworth has to be potentially capable of an act of apperception similar to what the poet presumably experienced in endowing, by a "certain colouring of imagination," the humblest "incidents and situations from common life" with an "unusual aspect." [43] The ideal end of the poem is to induce in the reader the structure of consciousness that makes it possible for the mean and the trivial to appear sublime.

Wordsworth's ambition is staggering, not only with respect to his readers but also with respect to the entire universe of perception, every last phenomenon of which can become transfigured. But this ambition ought to be seen as an explication of his own experience of imaginative consciousness, the programmatic result of his undeniable encounter with the facts of his own consciousness. It is his own power of imagination that he describes, in his note to "The Thorn," as "the faculty which produces impressive effects out of simple elements." [44] And because of this power, the supernatural powers of earlier orthodoxies no longer need to be invoked. Imagination, he writes in a letter to Southey, "does not require for its exercise the intervention of supernatural agency, but . . . may be called forth as imperiously, and for kindred results of pleasure, by incidents . . . in the humblest departments of daily life." [45] And Wordsworth's experience of the act of apperception latent in every act of perception is the ultimate source of that hope for a vision of a paradise to be regained in the "common day," a hope he describes in the "Prospectus" to *The Excursion:*

> Paradise, and groves
> Elysian, Fortunate Fields—like those of old
> Sought in the Atlantic Main—why should they be
> A history only of departed things,
> Or a mere fiction of what never was?
> For the discerning intellect of Man,
> When wedded to this goodly universe
> In love and holy passion, shall find these
> A simple produce of the common day.[46]

No divine intervention is required for the "common day" to be transfigured into a vision of paradise. And the poet's labor is to sing of "this great consummation" in words that "speak of nothing more than what we are." [47] Thus the paradox of *humilitas-sublimitas* extends even into Wordsworth's conception of the language appropriate for poetry, a language that ought to be derived, according to the well-known argument of the "Preface to the Lyrical Ballads," from the "real language" of humble and rustic men "in a state of vivid sensation." [48] Wordsworth's attack on "poetic diction" might be seen as an inevitable corollary of his ambition to transform the light of "common day" into the light of paradise. Such gaudy and "inane phraseology" is the analogue in language of those gaudy fictions "of what never was," those fictions of possible sublimity which are now to be dismissed. [49]

The poet, through the power of his own unaided mind, no longer needs to rely upon either discredited myth or discredited language from the past. Just as he can endow the humblest phenomenon with the appearance of sublimity, so he can use the humblest, most commonplace words in order to project his vision of a new Elysium of the here and now. Indeed, such language is far more appropriate for such a task since presumably in its very plainness it speaks "of nothing more than what we are." The vision of the new paradise of the "common day" requires a poet who will use the language of that day. Ideally, any word whatsoever, the "simple produce" of the common tongue, can become an "incarnation of the thought," an expressive embodiment of the act of sublime self-consciousness. For imagination has power to produce "impressive effects" out of the simplest of words.

In *The Prelude*, the story of the education of Wordsworth's mind at the hands of nature, the poet attributes to nature herself the power that he feels in his consciousness to make the humble sublime:

> Nature for all conditions wants not power
> To consecrate, if we have eyes to see,

The outside of her creatures, and to breathe
Grandeur upon the very humblest face
Of human life.[50]

These lines are but another expression of Wordsworth's characteristic displacement of consciousness into nature. This displacement allows Wordsworth to speak as if nature herself functioned in much the same way as his own creative mind. Nature can be taken as almost paradigmatic of poetic consciousness. In a curious reversal, therefore, Wordsworth can explicitly hope that the effect of his poetry will be similar to the effect that nature has upon those who "have eyes to see"—the effect that the displacement of his own consciousness into nature makes possible in the first place! Shortly after these lines in *The Prelude* he tells Coleridge of his desire that a work of his

Proceeding from the depth of untaught things,
Enduring and creative, might become
A power like one of Nature's.[51]

Wordsworth hopes for a poetry, in other words, which has that power, "like one of Nature's," to breathe "Grandeur upon the very humblest face / Of human life." But this breathing, this transforming function both of nature and of poetry, ultimately proceeds "from the depth of untaught things" inside the poet himself. For the paradox of *humilitas-sublimitas* takes its origin in that "depth" of subjectivity, that abyss of idealism, which is immediately intuited in the act of apperception. And such an intuition by its very nature can never be taught.

Not only is Wordsworth preoccupied with those "unassuming things, that hold / A silent station" in the world [52]—a concern prompted by his mission to extend the kingdom of the sublime—he is also preoccupied with the human virtue of humility as a necessary condition for the transfiguring act of the creative mind. The vision of a paradise of the here and the now is, to be sure, the result of the power of imagination projecting into the finite world the sublimity discovered "in the soul of Man." But the very possibility of that discovery seems in turn dependent upon the humility with respect to himself which the poet manages to sustain. Wordsworth, like Saint Bernard, seems to believe that humility is "the way which leads to truth"[53] and that the pursuit of vision depends, first of all, upon a continuing moral act. Hence Wordsworth's sustained fascination with those "among the walks of homely life" who are "men for contemplation framed"[54]—a group that includes the Wanderer of *The Excursion*, the leech-gather of "Resolution and Independence," and the blind beggar of Book VII of *The Prelude*. All these "Meek men" seem to Wordsworth to possess, or in some way to embody, an attitude toward the self that makes the act of vision possible. For, as he observes,

> How oft high service is performed within,
> When all the external man is rude in show,—
> Not like a temple rich with pomp and gold,
> But a mere mountain chapel, that protects
> Its simple worshippers from sun and shower.[55]

Again we see Wordsworth using images of dwelling-places—by now we have come to understand them as essentially images of immanent space—but here to characterize the humility of those natural visionaries, men always of lowly station, who populate his poetic landscape. For these meek men, totally devoid of any "pomp" about themselves, are able to engage in acts of "high service" within the mountain chapels of their own minds:

Theirs is the language of the heavens, the power,
The thought, the image, and the silent joy:
Words are but under-agents in their souls;

When they are grasping with their greatest strength,
They do not breathe among them.[56]

Humility seems to be the necessary condition for acts
of sublime self-consciousness, acts in which the mind
intuits an infinite reality that transcends the limits of
language itself. The "joy" of such a structure of consciousness is "silent" when that structure is not mediated by imagination's power to incarnate the "thought"
of the visionary mind in the inevitably limited and finite
bodies of words themselves. But why should humility
so dispose the mind toward vision? Perhaps because the
act of apperception is one in which the self, no longer
constituting itself as an object of thought, becomes
absolutely unconscious of any specific identity in terms
of which the self might define itself as distinct or separate from other identities. Pride therefore is not only
the antithesis of humility but also the antithesis of apperception. The proud man clings to himself as the
special object of his own thought. He is fascinated with
the "temple" of self which is "rich with pomp and gold."
And in this sustained fascination with an objectified
self, he prevents the active presence of his own consciousness from diffusing itself into the meanest flower
that blows in the phenomenal world. Pride cuts the
mind off from possible sublimity.

Thus Wordsworth's astonishing ambition as a poet
is ultimately rooted in an equally astonishing act of self-
forgetfulness. The poet shall gain his own life, and indeed a vision of the one life pervading the entire phenomenal world, only by losing his life, only by giving
up any sense of himself as a distinct and separate life
among other lives. The echoes of centuries of Christian
teaching upon the paradoxical means of self-transcen-
dence are obvious. But what finally marks Wordsworth
as distinctly beyond Christianity in both his poetic and
human hopes in his insistence upon the absolute isolation in which the visionary mind must work. The revela-

tion of the new paradise must be won without the help of divine intervention, without the ministry or sacraments of any church, without finally the help of his fellow man. As Wordsworth exclaims in the last book of *The Prelude,*

> Here must thou be, O Man!
> Power to thyself; no Helper hast thou here;
> Here keepest thou in singleness thy state:
> No other can divide with thee this work:
> No secondary hand can intervene
> To fashion this ability; 'tis thine,
> The prime and vital principle is thine
> In the recesses of thy nature, far
> From any reach of outward fellowship,
> Else is not thine at all.[57]

The act of visionary apperception is by its very nature beyond the helpful intervention of any "secondary hand." And only insofar as the poet intuits the "prime and vital principle" in the isolated "recesses" of his own mind, can he begin that work of transforming the humblest of appearances into a vision of a new paradise. In that work he also displays the autonomy of his own mind, a mind that by itself can undertake the labor of redemption without the "extraordinary" call of a Christian vocation. For poets, according to Wordsworth, are men who

> build up greatest things
> From least suggestions, ever on the watch,
> Willing to work and to be wrought upon,
> They need not extraordinary calls
> To rouze them, in a world of life they live,
> By sensible impressions not enthrall'd,
> But quicken'd, rouz'd, and made thereby more fit
> To hold communion with the invisible world.[58]

In "Tintern Abbey" we saw Wordsworth puzzling over the meaning of certain remembered acts of "communion with the invisible world," attempting to derive the proper conclusion from the undeniable fact of his having encountered a "something far more deeply interfused." In the oracular passages of the concluding book of *The Prelude*, we find Wordsworth insisting upon the power of unaided consciousness to elicit such "communion" out of the "least suggestions" provided by the world of perception. But, as I have argued throughout, this "communion" must finally be understood as indeed a form of self-communion whereby the poet apperceives the presence of his own consciousness at the very heart of every act of perception. Wordsworth is therefore by "sensible impressions not enthrall'd." His freedom is the freedom of a solitary mind to discover in the depths of his own subjectivity an infinite reality that far transcends the reality revealed in the act of perception. Like the hermit at the center of the landscape of "Tintern Abbey," Wordsworth's visionary mind sits alone, in a solitude of sublime self-consciousness which is both the ultimate threat to the world of perception and the exclusive source of that world's transfiguration.

Notes

Chapter 1: The Argument

1 *The Poetical Works of William Wordsworth,* ed. E. de Selincourt and Helen Darbishire, 2d ed. (Oxford, 1954), II, 261–262, lines 93–102. Hereafter this five-volume edition will be cited as *Poetical Works.*

2 For a statement of the traditional interpretation of "natural mysticism," see the introduction to Wordsworth's poems by Russell Noyes in his anthology *English Romantic Poetry and Prose* (New York, 1956), pp. 239–240.

3 Ernest Bernbaum observes that these "lines are commonly considered pantheistic." See his notes to the poem in the 3d ed. of his *Anthology of Romanticism* (New York, 1948), p. 1107. Noyes combines the reading of "pantheism" with his reading of "natural mysticism." The two characterizations are, of course, not a priori irreconcilable.

4 Saint Thomas Aquinas, for example, writes: "God is in all things, not, indeed, as part of their essence, nor as an accident, but as an agent is present to that upon which it acts. For an agent must be joined to that on which it acts immediately, and reach it by its power. . . . Now, since God is being itself by His own essence, created being must be His proper effect; as to ignite is the proper effect of fire. But God causes this effect in things not only when they first begin to be, but as long as they are preserved in being; as light is caused in the air by the sun as long as the air remains illuminated. Therefore, as long as a thing has being, so long must God be present to it, according to its mode of being. But being is innermost in each thing and most fundamentally present within all things. . . . Hence it must be that God is in all things, and innermostly." *Summa Theologica,* Part I, Q. 8, Art. 1. *Basic Writings of Saint Thomas Aquinas,* ed. Anton C. Pegis (New York, 1945), I, 63–64. The translation, as Pegis notes in his preface, is a revision by the editor of the English Dominican Translation by Father Laurence Shapcote.

5 Hopkins's version of immanence is mediated by Ignatian spirituality and by a belief in the eternal fact of the Incarnation. See his "Hurrahing in Harvest" for a good example of this mediation. For

an interesting comparison of Hopkins's approach to nature with Wordsworth's, see John Crowe Ransom's "William Wordsworth: Notes toward an Understanding of Poetry," *Wordsworth, Centenary Studies Presented at Cornell and Princeton Universities*, ed. Gilbert T. Dunklin (London, 1963), pp. 106–108.

[6] Saint Augustine, for example, writes: "Recognize in thyself something within, within thyself. Leave thou abroad both thy clothing and thy flesh; descend into thyself; go to thy secret chamber, thy mind. If thou be far from thine own self, how canst thou draw near unto God? For not in the body but in the mind was man made in the image of God. In his own similitude let us seek God: in his own image recognize the Creator." Quoted in *An Augustine Synthesis*, ed. Erich Przywara (New York, 1958), p. 18. No translator indicated.

[7] William Empson, in his *Seven Types of Ambiguity* (New York, 1955), finds these lines "muddled" and "shuffling" (p. 174). But perhaps Empson is led to this conclusion by his search for Wordsworth's "doctrine": "It is reasonable, then, to try to extract from this passage definite opinions on the relations of God, man, and nature, and on the means by which such relations can be known" (p. 172).

[8] For a discussion of the *anima mundi* in Wordsworth's thought, see the account by Raymond Dexter Havens in his *The Mind of a Poet* (Baltimore, 1941), I, 190–198.

[9] The Fenwick note reads in part: "To that dream-like vividness and splendour which invest objects of sight in childhood, every one, I believe, if he would look back, could bear testimony, and I need not dwell upon it here: but having in the Poem regarded it as presumptive evidence of a prior state of existence, I think it right to protest against a conclusion, which has given pain to some good and pious persons, that I meant to inculcate such a belief. It is far too shadowy a notion to be recommended to faith, as more than an element in our instincts of immortality. . . . Archimedes said that he could move the world if he had a point where on to rest his machine. Who has not felt the same aspirations as regards the world of his own mind? Having to wield some of its elements when I was impelled to write this Poem on the 'Immortality of the Soul,' I took hold of the notion of pre-existence as having sufficient foundation in humanity for authorizing me to make for my purpose the best use of it I could as a Poet." *Poetical Works*, IV, 463–464. As Wordsworth protests that he never "meant to inculcate such a belief," we hear, among other things, the voice of the orthodoxy of his old age. But the important point to note is how Wordsworth speaks here of the belief as a kind of symbolic form useful for structuring his experience of the "world of his own mind."

[10] Quoted by Pierre Thévenaz, "Reflexion and Consciousness of Self," *What is Phenomenology? and Other Essays*, ed. James M. Edie, trans. James M. Edie, Charles Courtney, Paul Brockelman (Chicago, 1962), p. 116. Here and occasionally elsewhere, where I use technical philosophical terms, I want it understood that I mean no more by them than what I make explicit in my text. I certainly do not

mean to carry into my essay the systematic demands or implications these terms might have in their original context. I also reserve the right to extend somewhat the meaning of these terms, always with explicit acknowledgment, when it suits my purpose.

[11] I assume of course that a memory has passed into a reexperiencing. See my comments (p. 1) on the implication of the shift in tense from "have felt" to "disturbs." For a discussion of this way of reading Wordsworth—of finding in a poem an immediately enacting consciousness—see sect. IV of this chapter. Donald Davie, in his *Articulate Energy* (New York, 1958), has a relevant observation. Speaking of the syntax of *The Prelude*—a syntax quite similar to that of "Tintern Abbey"—he notices that it "seems to be explaining, while in fact it is meditating, ruminating, at all events experiencing more fully than one does when one explains" (p. 111).

[12] From time to time throughout this study I shall support a point with an appeal to an etymology. I have no special theoretical case in support of this practice, merely a suspicion that an increasing sensitivity to the Latin origins of Wordsworth's occasionally Latinate diction will be illuminating—a suspicion that I hope will be pragmatically supported by the results of my practice. Certainly Wordsworth, with his classical training, was more sensitive to these roots than the average reader of today.

[13] Coleridge's object *qua* object always requires a subject, and thus can be identified with "intended object" which is always that which consciousness is conscious *of*. The question of whether this object, "intended" or Coleridge's object of a subject, is extramental is beside the point.

[14] *Wordsworth's Literary Criticism*, ed. Nowell C. Smith (London, 1905), p. 161 (hereafter cited as *Literary Criticism*). Italics mine.

[15] Empson, *The Structure of Complex Words* (Norfolk, Conn., 1951), p. 304.

[16] The question of the relationship between Wordsworth and the sublime has often been explored—and in a variety of contexts. See, for example, James Benzinger, *Images of Eternity* (Carbondale, Ill., 1962), pp. 52–64; J. T. Boulton, in the introduction to his edition of Burke's *A Philosophical Enquiry into the Origin of our Ideas of the Sublime and Beautiful* (New York, 1958), pp. xcvi, xcix–cii, lxxviii; A. C. Bradley, *Oxford Lectures on Poetry* (London, 1909), pp. 125–145; E. F. Carritt, *The Theory of Beauty*, 4th ed. (London, 1931), 220 f.; Havens, *The Mind of a Poet* (Baltimore, 1941), I, 39–51; James Scoggins, *Imagination and Fancy* (Lincoln, Neb., 1966), pp. 139–190. Other studies that have proved specifically helpful in my treatment of this question are noted, when appropriate, throughout the essay.

[17] "The Poet, described in *ideal* perfection, brings the whole soul of man into activity, with the subordination of its faculties to each other, according to their relative worth and dignity. He diffuses a tone and spirit of unity, that blends, and (as it were) *fuses*, each into each, by that synthetic and magical power, to which we have exclusively appropriated the name of imagination." Samuel Taylor

Coleridge, *Biographia Literaria*, ed. J. Shawcross (Oxford, 1907), II, 12 (hereafter cited as *Biographia*).

18 Hereafter I omit quotation marks around the word "sublime" except when the word is used *qua* word. By "sublime" I generally refer to the structure of consciousness that this essay investigates. Sometimes, however, the word will be used without quotation marks as an adjective to refer to the "sublime" object toward which consciousness is directed. The context should make clear when this is the case.

19 An excellent study of the development of this taste is Marjorie Hope Nicolson's *Mountain Gloom and Mountain Glory: The Development of the Aesthetics of the Infinite* (Ithaca, 1959).

20 Samuel H. Monk, *The Sublime: A Study of Critical Theories in Eighteenth-Century England* (New York, 1935). This work, the standard treatment of the subject, has proved invaluable in the preparation of this study.

21 Meyer Abrams, "English Romanticism: The Spirit of the Age," *Romanticism Reconsidered,* ed. Northrop Frye (New York, 1963), p. 64.

22 *Poetical Works,* V, 382–383, ll. 150–154. Italics mine.

23 Abrams observes that "it is astonishing how much of Coleridge's critical writing is couched in terms that are metaphorical for art and literal for a plant; if Plato's dialectic is a wilderness of mirrors, Coleridge's is a very jungle of vegetation." *The Mirror and the Lamp: Romantic Theory and the Critical Tradition* (New York, 1958), p. 169.

24 *Literary Criticism,* p. 129. I say "ideally" because Wordsworth in the same passage says that words can also be used as "only a clothing" for thought. But when so used, he goes on, they will "prove an ill gift."

25 In a very popular work of the late eighteenth century, Hugh Blair's *Lectures on Rhetoric and Belles Lettres* (1783), we find for example: "Simple expression just makes our idea known to others; but figurative language, over and above, bestows a particular dress upon that idea; a dress, which both makes it to be remarked, and adorns it" (Lecture XIV, "Figurative Language"). Quoted in *Essays on Rhetoric,* ed. Dudley Bailey (New York, 1965), p. 108.

26 John F. Danby, in his *William Wordsworth: The Prelude and Other Poems* (New York, 1963), has puzzled over the meaning the word "thought" ought to have in discussions of Wordsworth. He observes that for Wordsworth "a 'thought' is a movement of the mind when the mind is entering into and upon the self-constituting order-of-things" (p. 48). I accept the genus of Danby's definition: "thought" to be understood as "a movement of the mind."

27 *Literary Criticism,* p. 130.

28 Pope, "An Essay on Criticism," ll. 297–298.

29 And sometimes just such an implicit document. See Davie's observation quoted in n. 11. In the poem, in other words, we can see Wordsworth consciously reacting to, even reexperiencing, the history of his mind.

[30] Geoffrey Hartman, *Wordsworth's Poetry, 1787–1814* (New Haven, 1964).
[31] *Literary Criticism,* pp. 51–53.
[32] *Poetical Works,* III, 18.

CHAPTER 2: A POEM ABOUT INTERIORS

[1] Louis Martz, *The Poetry of Meditation,* rev. ed. (New Haven, 1962), p. 329.

[2] Albert S. Gérard, "Dark Passages: Exploring *Tintern Abbey*," *SIR,* III (1963), 22. David Ferry, in his *The Limits of Mortality* (Middletown, Conn., 1959), observes of the poem that it is "hard not to mistake for a confusion of feeling what may be a complexity of feeling, a contemplated and contained ambivalence" (pp. 110–111). Others who have proved helpful to me in preparing this reading are: Harold Bloom, *The Visionary Company: A Reading of English Romantic Poetry* (New York, 1963), pp. 149–159; Roger N. Murray, *Wordsworth's Style* (Lincoln, Neb., 1967), pp. 25–32; Christopher Salvesen, *The Landscape of Memory* (Lincoln, Neb., 1965), pp. 38–39; Carl Woodring, *Wordsworth* (Boston, 1965), pp. 59–64; and especially Geoffrey Hartman *Wordsworth's Poetry, 1787–1814* (New Haven, 1964), pp. 26–30, 175–176, *passim.*

[3] I use the word "immanent" in two slightly different senses throughout this essay: (1) to indicate "being within," as in "mind is immanent in nature"; (2) to indicate "have a 'within' or interior," as in "nature made immanent," i.e., made to have mind inside it. This second usage (far less frequent than the first) is prompted by Wordsworth's habit of obscuring the distinction between container and contained, indeed of reversing the roles without warning. Which of the two senses is intended should be clear from the context. In my analysis of what I later call Wordsworth's "language of immanence" I have been especially helped by C. C. Clarke's *Romantic Paradox* (New York, 1963), pp. 44–53.

[4] "The Drunken Boat: The Revolutionary Element in Romanticism," *Romanticism Reconsidered,* ed. Northrop Frye (New York, 1963), p. 16.

[5] Rudolf Otto, *The Idea of the Holy,* trans. John W. Harvey, 2d ed. (London, 1950). I introduce Otto's term for the sake of corroborating my connection between Wordsworth's act of visionary introspection (Frye's journey downward and inward) and the experience of awe and dread. According to Otto's phenomenology of religious consciousness, one of the essential characteristics of an encounter with a "numinous object" is the experience of "*mysterium tremendum.*" See Otto's analysis of "The Element of Awfulness," pp. 13–19. Wordsworth himself corroborates this connection in *The Recluse* lines cited in the text. The experience of "*mysterium tremendum*" is closely related to the feeling of a special kind of fear that many commentators have observed is a characteristic of the experience of the sublime, a relationship Otto himself notes (p. 42).

[6] G. W. Knight, *The Starlit Dome* (London, 1959), p. 11. Knight's study of "The Wordsworthian Profundity," pp. 1–82, is a brilliantly

suggestive treatment of the poet's fascination with depths, dwelling-places, and, in his later poems, architectural structures of all kinds; and in this respect corroborates the point of view taken in this chapter, i.e., regarding "Tintern Abbey" as a poem about interiors.

[7] *Poetical Works*, V, 4, ll. 35–41.

[8] For a discussion of Locke's metaphors of the mind, see *The Mirror and the Lamp*, pp. 57–58. Also see Ernest Lee Tuveson, *The Imagination as a Means of Grace* (Berkeley, 1960), p. 19.

[9] *The Prelude*, XIV, 194–196. All references to *The Prelude* are, unless otherwise indicated, to the 1850 version (book and line), ed. Ernest de Selincourt, 2d ed. rev. Helen Darbishire (Oxford, 1959).

[10] *The Prelude* (1805), XIII, 56, 62–65, 69. In the 1850 version (Book XIV) the explicit connection between imagination and the blue chasm disappears; the Snowdon scene is

> All meek and silent, save that through a rift—
> Not distant from the shore whereon we stood,
> A fixed, abysmal, gloomy, breathing-place—
> Mounted the roar of waters, torrents, streams
> Innumerable, roaring with one voice!
> Heard over earth and sea, and, in that hour,
> For so it seemed, felt by the starry heavens.
>
> [Ll. 56–62]

[11] *Ibid.* (1850), VI, 592–596. See Hartman's analysis of this episode, *Wordsworth's Poetry*, pp. 45–48.

[12] *The Prelude*, VI, 600–601.

[13] *Poetical Works*, V, 4, l. 57. This paragraph is especially indebted to Hartman's central thesis that Wordsworth, throughout his major poetry, exhibits a fear of what Hartman calls "apocalypse," i.e., the "death of nature."

[14] *The Prelude*, V, 45–49.

[15] Hartman, *Wordsworth's Poetry*, p. 173.

[16] Gaston Bachelard, in his *The Poetics of Space*, trans. Maria Jolas (New York, 1964), analyzes what he calls the "phenomenological reverberation" of the image of the hermit's hut as it is used in poetry. He offers a suggestive corroboration of the visionary implications I have been arguing attach to Wordsworth's image of the Hermit's cave: "The hermit's hut is an engraving that would suffer from any exaggeration of picturesqueness. Its truth must derive from the intensity of its essence, which is the essence of the verb 'to inhabit.' The hut immediately becomes centralized solitude, for in the land of legend, there exists no adjoining hut. . . . The image leads us on towards extreme solitude. The hermit is *alone* before God. His hut, therefore, is just the opposite of the monastery. And there radiates about this centralized solitude a universe of meditation and prayer, a universe outside the universe" (p. 32). In Wordsworth, of course, the "universe outside" is a "universe inside," and "centralized solitude" is the condition of the mind's encountering its own powers.

17 Wordsworth's sense of, and language of, space is not confined to his own practice but seems to be one of the commonplaces of the Romantic Period. Thomas De Quincey, for example, offers what could almost be taken as a paradigm for the kind of reading I am pursuing: "Great is the mystery of Space, greater is the mystery of Time. Either mystery grows upon man as man himself grows; and either seems to be a function of the godlike which is in man. In reality, the depths and the heights which are in man, the depths by which he searches, the heights by which he aspires, are but projected and made objective externally in the three dimensions of space which are outside of him. He trembles at the abyss into which his bodily eyes look down, or look up; not knowing that abyss to be, not always consciously suspecting it to be, but by an instinct written in his prophetic heart feeling it to be, boding it to be, fearing it to be, and sometimes hoping it to be, the mirror to a mightier abyss that will one day be expanded in himself" (*Collected Writings,* ed. David Masson, 14 vols. [London, 1896, 1897], VIII, 15).

18 *Poetical Works,* II, 517. I use the term "antistrophe" (Gk. *antistrephein,* to turn against or opposite) in somewhat of a Romantic way: to refer to a movement of the mind rather than to a stanza in the traditional "sublime ode." The usage is suggested by Wordsworth's note.

19 The introspective act described by Wordsworth in the second verse paragraph is, in certain respects, similar to one of the ways in which a man might pursue, in Addisonian terms, the "pleasures of the imagination." Addison writes in *The Spectator,* no. 411, how by "this Faculty a Man in a Dungeon is capable of entertaining himself with Scenes and Landskips more beautiful than any that can be found in the whole Compass of Nature." Addison of course would probably disallow Wordsworth's claim that in his city dungeon he saw into the "life of things": the imagination, to be sure, can give great pleasure, but to say that it is capable of such metaphysical insight is to allow the pursuit of imagination's pleasures to turn into a dangerous form of enthusiasm. Is Wordsworth here vaguely troubled by the possible charge of enthusiasm? In any case, Wordsworth's "antistrophe" is related to what Robert Langbaum, in "Romanticism as a Modern Tradition," *A Grammar of Literary Criticism,* ed. Lawrence Sargent Hall (New York, 1965), has said is a recurring problem of many Romantic moments of "illumination": "As an experience, the illumination is undeniably valid. But once the perception of value is abstracted from the immediate experience and formulated for application elsewhere, it becomes mere theory and therefore problematical" (p. 255). For a recent study of the Romantic problem of experience vs. formulation, as this problem is worked out in a single poem, see Bernard J. Paris, "Coleridge's 'The Eolian Harp'," *PMASAL,* LI (1966), 571–582.

20 An anchor is also the traditional symbol of hope. Saint Paul establishes the equation in Hebrews 6:19: "hope we have as an anchor of the soul, both sure and steadfast, and which entereth into that within the veil" (King James Version). In English poetry examples of this traditional emblem can be found in George Herbert's

145

"Hope" and in Spenser's portrait of Speranza in Book I, Canto X, xiv, *The Faerie Queene*. In "Tintern Abbey," just as Wordsworth meditates his way toward a pledge of continuing faith in nature, so also he is seeking grounds for a continuing sense of hope: he dares "to hope" in line 65. In terms of traditional symbolism to "anchor" one's "purest thoughts" in "nature and the language of the sense" is to posit a purely sensationalistic ground for hope—an extraordinary reversal of the Christian grounding of hope in the world beyond. Note also how Saint Paul's metaphor of hope as that "which entereth into that within the veil" suggests a movement into a transcendent interior (his vehicle, of course, is the veil of the Jewish temple). Likewise, in Herbert's poem personified Hope presents the poet with an "optick" or telescope, a means of penetrating otherwise hidden spaces. These associations become even more provocative if we regard Wordsworth's counting of the "gifts" he has received from nature as a secularized version of a traditional meditation recommended for those tempted by despair. Jeremy Taylor, for example, gives as his ninth "remedy" against despair the directive: "Gather together into your spirit and its treasure-house the memory, not only all the promises of God, but also the remembrances of experience and the former senses of the Divine favours, that from thence you may argue from times past to the present, and enlarge to the future and to greater blessings. For although the conjectures and expectations of hope are not like the conclusions of faith, yet they are a helmet against the scorching of despair in temporal things, and an anchor of the soul, sure and steadfast, against the fluctuations of the spirit in matters of the soul" (*The Rule and Exercises of Holy Living*, ed. Thomas S. Kepler [New York, 1956], p. 160). I am not suggesting "source" or "influence," but certainly Wordsworth's oblique echoing of these traditions suggests that an illuminating reading of the poem might be developed by regarding it as a meditation principally concerned with the problem of hope—a suggestion enforced when we recall that the longest poem published by Wordsworth during his lifetime, *The Excursion*, has as its central theme the correction of despondency or despair. Two final observations: (1) the prevailing color of the landscape of Tintern Abbey is green, another traditional emblem of hope; (2) in Book VI of *The Prelude*, at the moment of Wordsworth's unmediated contact with imagination rising from the mind's abyss, the poet claims to see, among other things, that

> our being's heart and home
> Is with infinitude, and only there;
> With hope it is, hope that can never die.
> [Ll. 604–606]

The vision provided by his encounter with imagination, in other words, reveals the grounds of hope. In "Tintern Abbey" Wordsworth decides that "nature and the language of the sense" will be his anchor immediately *after* his encounter with the transcendent "something." It goes without saying that the parallel is striking: in "Tintern

Abbey" Wordsworth searches through the dwelling-places of nature to a "sense sublime" of the activity of his own consciousness, i.e., the act of imagination.

21 *The Prelude*, XII, 272–273, 277–280.

22 In sect. IV of this chapter I deliberately abandon the use of the term "imagination." Up to this point I have been employing the term freely because I have been attempting to trace indications of certain features of what I have called Wordsworth's "geography of introspection"; and from that point of view it seemed necessary to say—led on by the example of Wordsworth's own metaphors—that imagination is encountered by the act of introspection in the depths of subjectivity. In the concluding analysis of sect. IV, however, I try to shift my terms away from metaphor toward greater precision. The reader is asked to assume that I intend a rough equation between "the act of reflexive self-awareness" and "the act of imagination." The grounds of this equation, which I explore in the next chapter, are exceedingly intricate, and cannot be faced now without muddling somewhat the analysis of the poem. To avoid this muddle, I momentarily suspend my use of the term "imagination," and ask my reader's patience. Hartman occasionally uses the term "imagination" as almost a synonym for "self-consciousness." He does not, in my judgment, sufficiently distinguish between what I call in sect. IV "thinking about" the self, i.e., constituting the subject as an object for thought, and what I call "reflexive self-awareness" or "apperception," i.e., becoming conscious of the activity of the subject's consciousness *without* the subject's constituting this activity as an object of consciousness. This distinction is related to one of the central questions of modern phenomenology: whether the subject can become aware of the subject *qua* subject without losing itself as an object of thought. See Pierre Thévenaz's discussion of this "Charybdis and Scylla" of introspection in *What is Phenomenology?*, esp. pp. 113–115.

23 *The Prelude* (1805), XIII, 108–111.

24 Cf. the implication of Donne's "Who sees God's face, that is self life, must die" ("Good Friday, 1613," l. 17).

25 *Poetical Works*, IV, 283, ll. 130–131.

26 Kenneth Burke, *A Grammar of Motives and A Rhetoric of Motives* (New York, 1962), p. 24. From this Burkean point of view we might also suggest that the previously noticed complaint by Wordsworth about the inadequacy of the frail lodges of nature is, among other things, a complaint about the inadequacy of nature as a language whereby to express the reality of his mind. In Book V of *The Prelude* Wordsworth sees the language of poetry as a "mansion" (like the dwelling-places of nature?) which embodies "Visionary power" and "the host of shadowy things" (ll. 595–600). We noted in the introductory chapter how words, according to Wordsworth, ideally should be an "incarnation" of thought. If nature is also to provide a "language," then of course it too ideally should be an "incarnation" of thought, i.e., of the visionary underworld.

CHAPTER 3: THE EXTENSIONS OF CONSCIOUSNESS

1 *The Prelude*, p. 483.

² A selective bibliography of these previous examinations is given in n. 16 to chap. 1.

³ Brief discussions of the relationship between Burke's theory of the sublime and Wordsworth can be found in Raymond Dexter Havens, *The Mind of a Poet* (Baltimore, 1941), I, 47–48, 52–53; and in J. T. Boulton's introduction to his edition of Edmund Burke's *A Philosophical Enquiry into the Origin of our Ideas of the Sublime and Beautiful* (New York, 1958), pp. xcix–cii.

My exclusion of Burke from this chapter is not intended to deny the possibility of a phenomenological mediation between Burke's "aesthetics of terror" and Wordsworth's experience of the sublime. Certainly my discussion of Wordsworthian "awe" in the previous chapter is suggestive in this direction. Such a mediation, however, can only be made on a very high level of phenomenological abstraction, a level that will enable us to overlook the explicit sensationalism of Burke's theory. I suggest that an approach to the problem might be developed out of an analysis of what Burke means when he speaks of that "delightful terror" which for him is the essential ingredient of the experience of the sublime. This terror, according to Burke, is of a very special kind. It ought not to be confused with the terror aroused because of an immediate and seemingly inescapable threat to one's well-being. Burke indicates this distinction in his observation that when "danger or pain press too nearly, they are incapable of giving any delight, and are simply terrible; but at certain distances, and with certain modifications, they may be, and they are delightful" (Burke, *A Philosophical Enquiry*, p. 40). In other words, the terror of the sublime must be mediated by a simultaneous recognition that the self is not *really* about to be destroyed: the terror ought not to be "conversant about the present destruction of the person" (p. 136). Such a terror is thus related to those "Passions belonging to self-preservation" which Burke claims to be the "strongest of all the passions" (p. 51). And such a terror can be characterized by Burke as "delightful" because, as he tells us early in his *Enquiry*, he thinks the word "delight" ought to be used "to express the sensation which accompanies the removal of pain or danger" (p. 37). For Burke, it would therefore seem, the experience of the sublime is curiously double, involving both a painful sense of the potential destruction of the self and a delightful sense of security, a sense of the self's "removal" from the imminence of death.

Now, if we go on to characterize this structure of consciousness as essentially dialectical—a curiously intense mixture of a sense of personal danger and mortality with a sense of personal transcendence —we are in a position, I think, to approach Wordsworth. The dialectic of this phenomenological polarity seems to be involved in a number of the poet's more memorable experiences. I think especially of the "spots of time" passages in *The Prelude* which so often tell of Wordsworth's encountering the terrible and the threatening and *at the same time* somehow finding implicit in these encounters a sense of the power of his own mind to attain to a visionary state in which the fear of personal danger is overcome. One way of looking at "Resolution and Independence" might be to see it as a poem that tells of the movement of the poet's mind from an anguished preoccupation with thoughts of death to a state in which, because of the strangely visionary resonances of the leech-gatherer, the fear of death is transformed into a triumphant sense of man's ability to live in spite of the encroachments of mortality. Perhaps the leech-gatherer, as a living emblem both of the terrible ravages of time and of a man's power to resist these ravages, might be taken as a visible expression of that dialectical structure of consciousness in which the terrors of annihilation are transformed into a sense of secure endurance. And perhaps, therefore, it is Wordsworth's chance meeting with the leech-gatherer which provides the poet with what might be called a living emotional paradigm in terms of which he can organize his own emotions and finally stabilize himself in the face of his own fear of death.

4 My exploration of this relationship is not to be taken as a specific "source" or "influence" study. I am not at all concerned with pinpointing certain historical "causalities," that is, with showing how something in Wordsworth might be regarded as an influenced "effect" of some historically given "cause"—the work, for example, of an earlier poet or critic or philosopher. It is one thing to locate the Wordsworthian sensibility with reference to an historically given body of speculation. It is quite another thing to argue direct historical "source" or "influence."

5 Ernst Lee Tuveson, *The Imagination as a Means of Grace* (Berkeley and Los Angeles, 1960), p. 105.

6 John Baillie, *An Essay on the Sublime,* The Augustan Reprint Society, No. 43 (Los Angeles, 1953), p. 4. Originally published in London in 1747.

7 Joseph Priestley, *A Course of Lectures on Oratory and Criticism* (London, 1777), p. 151.

8 Alexander Gerard, *An Essay on Taste,* 3d ed. (Edinburgh, 1780), p. 12.

9 David Hume, *A Treatise of Human Nature,* ed. L. A. Selby-Bigge (Oxford, 1888), p. 432.

10 *The Spectator,* no. 412; italics mine. Monk points out that for Addison greatness "is identical with sublimity" (*The Sublime: A Study of Critical Theories in Eighteenth-Century England* [New York, 1935], p. 57).

11 Walter J. Ong, S.J., would probably see in this use of spatial metaphors but another manifestation of the tendency to conceptualize mental operations in terms of visual and spatial analogies, a tendency that, he argues, begins to dominate Western thinking about thinking with the quantification of late medieval logic. See his "System, Space, and Intellect in Renaissance Symbolism," *The Barbarian Within* (New York, 1962), pp. 68–85. Certainly British eighteenth-century empiricism is dominated by the Lockean conception of thinking as a kind of seeing. This analogy can be seen explicitly working in Hume's description of the moral judgment: "It has been observ'd, that nothing is ever present to the mind but its perceptions; and that all the actions of seeing, hearing, judging, loving, hating and thinking, fall under this denomination. The mind can never exert itself in any ac-

tion, which we may not comprehend under the term of perception; and consequently that term is no less applicable to those judgments, by which we distinguish moral good and evil, than to every other operation of the mind. To approve of one character, to condemn another, are only so many different perceptions" (*A Treatise of Human Nature*, p. 456). For Hume, it would seem, the metaphor of thinking as a kind of seeing is universal in its applicability to the analysis of consciousness: "For my part, when I enter most intimately into what I call *myself*, I always stumble on some particular perception or other, of heat or cold, light or shade, love or hatred, pain or pleasure. I never can catch *myself* at any time without a perception, and never can observe any thing but the perception" (p. 252). It might be argued that implicit in this last statement by Hume—and perhaps implicit in the whole British empirical psychology committed as it was to the Lockean analogy of thinking as a kind of seeing—is the impossibility of any adequate theory of apperception, of any theory of the subject grasping the subject *qua* subject. Reflexive consciousness for Hume would logically always have to be thought of as an object being seen. In the act of introspection, in other words, the self would always have to be perceived; it could never be apperceived. Now from this point of view—and granting the thesis of this essay, namely, that for Wordsworth the activity of his imagination is grounded in an act of apperception—we should not be surprised to find the poet moving toward the visionary as he moves from images of the eye to "images" of the ear: precisely the action of the first stanza of "The Solitary Reaper." Nor should we be surprised that Wordsworth is frequently preoccupied, as he tries to explain poetic consciousness, with dark, open-ended spaces or with unseen, dislocated sounds. Both sets of phenomena might be taken as the poet's expressive vehicles of a consciousness grasping itself as an active subject, and refusing to transform itself into a "visible" object of perception. Wordsworth's preoccupation with "immanence" —discussed in the previous chapter—thus might further be understood as a search for a way of conceptualizing consciousness in a manner undreamt of in Locke's philosophy: the unseen depths of visible things are emblematic of those operations of the mind which cannot be explained according to Locke's basic analogy without their being explained out of existence. From this point of view we might further understand why, as I state at the conclusion of the previous chapter, Wordsworth's "God" must be as hidden, i.e., as unseen, as Saint Paul's.

12 Ernst Cas. irer, *The Philosophy of Symbolic Forms, Volume Three: The Phenomenology of Knowledge*, trans. Ralph Manheim (New Haven, 1957), p. 144.

13 For a discussion of the theoretical difficulties of Cartesian dualism, see Basil Willey's *The Seventeenth Century Background* (New York, 1953), pp. 89–91. Of course sublime consciousness, as described at this point in my essay, offers no theoretical solution to the problems of dualism.

14 Gerard, *Essay on Taste*, p. 12.

15 *The Spectator*, no. 420.

16 *The Prelude*, III, 63. From the point of view of the history of

ideas, it is indeed appropriate that Wordsworth applies these words to Newton who of course, more than any other thinker, "created" the infinite space cited by theorists of the sublime.

[17] *Poetical Works*, IV, 463.

[18] Cassirer, *Philosophy of Symbolic Forms*, III, 143.

[19] Tuveson, *Imagination as a Means of Grace*, p. 105.

[20] *Principia* (Berkeley, 1947), p. 545.

[21] Shaftesbury, *Characteristics* (London, 1787), II, 343, 345.

[22] Longinus, *On Great Writing (On the Sublime)*, trans. G. M. A. Grube, The Library of Liberal Arts, no. 79 (New York, 1957), p. 10.

[23] Baillie, *Essay on the Sublime*, p. 7.

[24] *Ibid.*, p. 4.

[25] *Ibid.*

[26] *Ibid.*, p. 6.

[27] The same tendency to explain the quality of a mind in quantitative terms can be found in the following remarks of John Dennis: "Men are mov'd for two Reasons, either because they have weak Minds and Souls, that are capable of being mov'd by little Objects and consequently by little and ordinary Ideas; or because they have Greatness of Soul and Capacity, to discern and feel the great ones; for the Enthusiastick Passions being caus'd by the Ideas, it follows, that the more the Soul is capable of receiving Ideas whose Objects are truly great and wonderful, the greater will the enthusiasm be that is caus'd by those Ideas. From whence it follows, that the greater the Soul is, and the larger the Capacity, the more will it be mov'd by religious ideas" (*The Grounds of Criticism in Poetry, in Critical Works*, ed. Edward Niles Hooker [Baltimore, 1939–1943], I, 340).

[28] Edward Young, *Night Thoughts*, IX, ll. 913–914, 1013–1014.

[29] Gerard, *Essay on Taste*, p. 12.

[30] Hume, *Treatise*, pp. 433–434.

[31] *Ibid.*, p. 436.

[32] Priestley, *Course of Lectures*, p. 151.

[33] *The Prelude* (1805), VII, 718–720.

[34] Certainly for Baillie simplicity is a desired characteristic of the sublime: "The *Sublime*, when it exists *simple* and unmixed, by filling the *Mind* with one *vast and uniform Idea*, affects it with a solemn *Sedateness;* by this means the Soul itself becomes, as it were, one *simple grand Sensation*" (*Essay on the Sublime*, p. 33). Burke states quite categorically that he knows "of nothing sublime which is not some modification of power" (*Philosophical Enquiry*, p. 64).

[35] *The Prelude* (1805), VII, 721–726.

[36] Since Wordsworth so often speaks of the eternity of the mind, I see no distortion in equating, as I do here, the term "mind" and the term "soul." It can generally be said that "mind" in Wordsworth, when seen under the aspect of its own eternity, is frequently characterized by the poet as "soul."

[37] The paradigmatic and revelatory function of natural phenomena is quite explicitly described in these lines from the 1850 *Prelude:*

> Think, how the everlasting streams and woods,
> Stretched and still stretching far and wide, exalt
> The roving Indian, on his desert sands:

What grandeur not unfelt, what pregnant show
Of beauty, meets the sun-burnt Arab's eye:
And, as the sea propels, from zone to zone,
Its currents; magnifies its shoals of life
Beyond all compass; spreads, and sends aloft
Armies of clouds,—even so, its powers and aspects
Shape for mankind, by principles as fixed,
The views and aspirations of the soul
To majesty.

[VII, 745–756]

(De Selincourt—or perhaps it was Wordsworth—mispunctuates in l. 748. The colon seems properly to belong after "roving Indian," leaving "on his desert sands" to the sun-burnt Arab.)

38 *The Excursion*, I, 77–80, 108. All references to this poem are to the version appearing in volume V of *Poetical Works*.

39 *Ibid.*, ll. 127–129, 132, 135–139.

40 *Ibid.*, ll. 140–142.

41 *Ibid.*, ll. 144–148.

42 *Poetical Works*, V, 13.

43 The ambiguities of the term "image" in Wordsworth's poetry is one of the central preoccupations of C. C. Clarke's *Romantic Paradox* (New York, 1963).

44 De Selincourt's note is helpful here: "It is generally stated that the images of dreams are vague and indistinct and lack colour. W.'s experience was the opposite" (*Poetical Works*, V, 411).

45 *The Excursion*, I, 154–155, 160–163.

46 *Ibid.*, ll. 223–225.

47 *Ibid.*, ll. 226–234.

48 Another way of understanding how the Pedlar finds "evidence" for his immortality by contemplating the mountains' sublime forms might be developed through an analysis of the phenomenological affinities between sublime consciousness and what Cassirer calls "mythical consciousness." Such a consciousness, according to Cassirer, "refuses to draw a distinction which is not inherent in the immediate content of experience, but which results only from reflection on the empirical *conditions* of life, that is, from a specific form of *causal analysis* . . . all reality is taken only as it is given in the immediate impression." Thus, for such an "undifferentiated" and "unreflecting" consciousness, it "is not immortality, but mortality that must be 'proved,' i.e., that must little by little be ascertained theoretically, through dividing lines which progressive reflection draws in the content of immediate experience" (*The Philosophy of Symbolic Forms, Volume Two: Mythical Thought*, trans. Ralph Manheim [New Haven, 1955], 37). Now, if we recall that according to eighteenth-century theorists one of the principal effects of the sublime is "astonishment," and if we accept Burke's not untypical description of astonishment as that "state of the soul" in which "the mind is so entirely filled with its object, that it cannot entertain any other, nor by consequence reason on that object which employs it" (*Philosophical Enquiry*, p. 57), then we might argue that sublime consciousness is similar to

mythical consciousness in at least this one respect: both involve structures of consciousness in which, in the words of Cassirer, "all reality is taken only as it is given in the immediate impression." For neither kinds of consciousness, therefore, is there the possibility of those "reflections on the empirical *conditions* of life" which can lead to the judgment that beyond the vividness of the "immediate impression" is the prospect of death. The Pedlar in the mountains, in other words, is "astonished" into a mythical structure of consciousness in which the idea of his own death is impossible. Likewise, the mountains are seen as "eternal" because the reflective judgment that they might indeed have an end in time is not possible for that state of subjective awareness which these mountains elicit in consciousness. Obviously the analogies that might be drawn between sublime consciousness and mythical consciousness deserve careful analysis, especially with reference to Wordsworth whose most sincerely felt religious pronouncements quite frequently grow out of mental experiences he himself characterizes as "sublime." Obvious also is the necessity of finding some way of accommodating the analogy sketched here to the Burkean position that the experience of the sublime involves a vivid intuition of the mortality of the subject. See n. 3 of this chapter.

49 The notion that in the experience of the sublime the fancy or the imagination is stirred to some sort of answering action is a commonplace found in many eighteenth-century commentaries. Perhaps the notion grows out of Longinus's remark that one of the tests of the rhetorical sublime is whether the passage in question provokes in the mind of the reader "reflections which reach beyond what was said" (*On Great Writing*, p. 10). In Archibald Alison's *Essays on the Nature and Principles of Taste*, 5th ed. (Edinburgh, 1817), we find the observation that the true experiencing of sublime emotion is not possible unless "our imagination is seized, and our fancy busied in the pursuit of all those trains of thought" which should have been awakened by the original perception of the sublime object (I, 5).

50 *Literary Criticism*, p. 161. We can note how for Wordsworth these actions of the imagination are themselves productive of the sublime. He writes, in his *Guide through the District of the Lakes*, ed. W. M. Merchant (London, 1951), that "sublimity will never be wanting, where the sense of innumerable multitude is lost in, and alternates with that of intense unity" (p. 123).

51 *Literary Criticism*, p. 162. Coleridge sees a similar relationship between the Hebrews and sublimity: "Could you ever discover anything sublime in our sense of the term, in the classic Greek literature? Sublimity is Hebrew by birth." *Table Talk and Omniana*, ed. T. Ashe (London, 1884), p. 174.

52 *The Prelude* (1805), XIII, 106–107, 108–111.

53 And insofar as Wordsworth's metaphors are of a space that is dark and open-ended (or immanent), they in fact present a mind that cannot be visualized, or converted into an object of thought as if it were an object of some inner "perception." See n. 11 of this chapter.

54 *Literary Criticism*, pp. 163–164.

CHAPTER 4: THE INTUITION OF EXISTENCE

1 The most helpful general treatment of the Coleridgean sublime is Clarence DeWitt Thorpe's "Coleridge on the Sublime" in *Wordsworth and Coleridge,* ed. Earl Leslie Griggs (New York, 1962), pp. 192–219. This chapter covers much of the same evidence Thorpe examines. But my focus is much narrower than his in that I am primarily concerned with working out the phenomenological implications of the fact that for Coleridge, as Thorpe himself points out, sublimity is inherently subjective. Thorpe's article should be consulted for the sake of the broader perspective he brings to bear upon the whole question of the Coleridgean sublime.

2 *Ibid.,* p. 212.

3 J. Shawcross, "Coleridge Marginalia," *N&Q,* IV (October 1905), 342. Words in brackets suggested by Shawcross to fill a hiatus in the MS.

4 Ernst Cassirer, *The Philosophy of Symbolic Forms, Volume Three: The Phenomenology of Knowledge,* trans. Ralph Manheim (New Haven, 1957), p. 143.

5 "Unpublished Fragments on Aesthetics by S. T. Coleridge," ed. Thomas M. Raysor, *NCUSP,* XXII (1925), 533.

6 *Coleridge's Miscellaneous Criticism,* ed. Thomas M. Raysor (Cambridge, 1936), pp. 11–12.

7 It might be argued that the statement "I am nothing!" should be taken to mean very simply: "I feel very small in comparison with the infinity and vastness suggested by a Gothic cathedral." The reading, however, is at odds with the spatial implications of Coleridge's statement that he feels *himself,* his "whole being," expanding "into the infinite." More important, this reading is at odds with Coleridge's observation discussed later in this chapter that the experience of sublimity suspends the comparing powers of the mind.

8 *The Friend,* 4th ed. (London, 1850), I, 134–135.

9 In this matter Coleridge echoes Burke, who in his *Enquiry* speaks of "the force of a judicious obscurity" in evoking feelings of sublimity, and who also remarks that "there are reasons in nature why the obscure idea . . . should be more affecting than the clear. It is our ignorance of things that causes all our admiration, and chiefly excites our passions. . . . The ideas of eternity, and infinity, are among the most affecting we have, and yet perhaps there is nothing of which we really understand so little, as of infinity and eternity" (Edmund Burke, *A Philosophical Enquiry into the Origin of our Ideas of the Sublime and Beautiful,* pp. 59, 61).

10 "Unpublished Fragments on Aesthetics," pp. 532–533.

11 Another way of putting all this is suggested by Coleridge's general description of a symbol as characterized "above all by the translucence of the eternal through and in the temporal" (*The Statesman's Manual,* in *Works,* ed. W. G. T. Shedd [New York, 1884], I, 437). The sublime circle might be said to exhibit a translucence of the shapeless through and in the shapely. But the "shapeless" which becomes *translucent* in this instance is, paradoxically enough, the *obscure* and indefinite idea of eternity.

Perhaps we come closer to an understanding of this paradox if we generally characterize the Coleridgean symbol in Miltonic language as a kind of "darkness visible." For Coleridge the idea of the "eternal" would always have to be an "obscure" idea since it is inevitably an "indefinite" idea. Extending his metaphor of "translucence," therefore, we might say that the symbol is characterized by a shining of the darkness of the idea of the eternal through and in something temporal and visible. Now it seems to me that these paradoxes partially grow out of the habit of British empirical psychology after Locke of discussing thinking as a kind of seeing, and therefore of discussing ideas as if they were somehow objects of sight. (See n. 11, chap. 3.) Coleridge himself, in his attack on Hartley in the *Biographia,* complains of the "despotism of the eye" and of how "under this strong sensuous influence, we are restless because invisible things are not the objects of vision; and metaphysical systems, for the most part, become popular, not for their truth, but in proportion as they attribute to causes a susceptibility of being seen, if only our visual organs were sufficiently powerful" (*Biographia,* I, 74). Yet when Coleridge uses the term "translucence" in his explanation of the symbol, it would seem as if he has not quite escaped the Lockean habit. Or perhaps—to put this more precisely—we might say that his metaphor of "translucence" is an attempt to mediate between the Lockean way of discussing ideas as if they were objects of sight and his own belief that certain ideas cannot be so explained, that certain ideas ought not to be submitted to the "despotism of the eye." In phenomenological terminology, we might say that consciousness, when it is directed toward a Coleridgean symbol, simultaneously intends two ideas in a single act: one idea may be discussed in terms appropriate to an object of sight (as, for example, the idea of a circle); the other cannot be so discussed (as, for example, the idea of eternity). One idea might be said to have a "shape," the other is "shapeless." According to Coleridge, therefore, the symbol-making power of the mind implicitly refutes a basic methodological assumption of Lockean epistemology; but his use of the term "translucence" almost conceals this refutation.

Likewise, when I speak in my text of how the "image of the circle as objectively shapely recedes, as it were, into the obscurity of the idea of eternity," I engage in a somewhat Lockean manner of speaking: attempting to discuss a certain act of consciousness in language appropriate to the act of seeing. Since, finally, this act cannot be fully analyzed in such language, my phrasing becomes as implicitly paradoxical as Coleridge's use of the term "translucence."

[12] *Coleridge's Miscellaneous Criticism,* p. 164.

[13] *Unpublished Letters of Samuel Taylor Coleridge,* ed. Earl Leslie Griggs (London, 1932), I, 117.

[14] In this sentence I explicitly fall back upon spatial metaphors in an attempt to make myself clear. Sometimes it seems impossible to discuss these matters without such verbal strategies. The methodological problem is recognized by Coleridge himself in his comments on Wordsworth's "Immortality Ode": "the ode was intended for such readers only as had been accustomed to watch the flux and reflux of their inmost nature, to venture at times into the twilight realms of

consciousness, and to feel a deep interest in modes of inmost being, to which they know that the attributes of time and space are inapplicable, and alien, but which yet can not be conveyed save in symbols of time and space" (*Biographia*, II, 120).

15 *The Notebooks of Samuel Taylor Coleridge*, ed. Kathleen Coburn (New York, 1962), I, 921.

16 "Coleridge Marginalia," p. 341.

17 Thorpe, "Coleridge on the Sublime," p. 215.

18 *The Friend*, III, 192–193.

19 *Ibid.*, pp. 193, 200.

20 *Biographia*, II, 47.

21 Etienne Gilson, *History of Christian Philosophy in the Middle Ages* (New York, 1955), pp. 368–369.

22 *The Friend*, III, 202.

23 *Ibid.*, p. 201.

24 Coleridge's notion that the experience of sublimity suspends the comparative powers of the mind seems to be a refinement of the commonplace assertion by eighteenth-century theorists that one of the principal effects of the sublime is a feeling of "astonishment." Burke describes this "state of the soul" as one in which "the mind is so entirely filled with its object, that it cannot entertain any other, nor by consequence reason upon that object which employs it" (*Enquiry*, p. 57). We might also say, therefore, that Coleridge's intuition of absolute existence provokes astonishment; it is an intuition that "admits of no question out of itself."

25 Cited by Shawcross in the notes to his edition of the *Biographia*, II, 309.

26 *Ibid.*

27 *Ibid.*

28 Further corroboration of my assertion that the intuition is derived from a special form of introspection is implied in the following. Coleridge is wondering about the origin of the intuition: "In vain would we derive it from the organs of sense: for these supply only surface, undulations, phantoms. In vain from the instruments of sensation: for these furnish only the chaos, the shapeless elements of sense. And least of all may we hope to find its origin, or sufficient cause, in the moulds and mechanism of the understanding, the whole purport and functions of which consist in individualization, in outlines and differencings by quantity and relation. It were wiser to seek substance in shadow, than absolute fulness in mere negation. . . . To no class of phænomena or particulars can it be referred, itself being none; therefore, to no faculty by which these alone are apprehended. As little dare we refer it to any form of abstraction or generalization; for it has neither co-ordinate nor *analogon;* it is absolute one; and that it is, and affirms itself to be, is its only predicate" (*The Friend*, III, 194).

29 *Ibid.*, p. 193.

30 *The Prelude* (1805), II, 416–434.

31 *Literary Criticism*, pp. 173, 199.

32 *Ibid.*, pp. 18, 28. Italics mine.

33 *Notebooks*, II, 3158.
34 *Biographia*, I, 202.
35 *Ibid.*
36 *Notebooks*, II, 2057.
37 *The Prelude*, VI, 592–596.
38 *Ibid.*, ll. 600–602.
39 *Ibid.*, l. 602.
40 *Ibid.*, ll. 624–640.
41 Another significant moment of "hanging" can be found in Book I
of *The Prelude*. And here again, I believe, we have a description suggestive of a dangerous balance between the phenomenal world and visionary consciousness:

> Oh! when I have hung
> Above the raven's nest, by knots of grass
> And half-inch fissures in the slippery rock
> But ill sustained, and almost (so it seemed)
> Suspended by the blast that blew amain,
> Shouldering the naked crag, oh, at that time
> While on the perilous ridge I hung alone,
> With what strange utterance did the loud dry wind
> Blow through my ear! the sky seemed not a sky
> Of earth—and with what motion moved the clouds!
>
> [Ll. 330–339]

It is significant that such experiences should have been part of the education of the mind of that poet whose imaginative task is, as he himself defines it, to provide "sensuous incarnation" for the "ethereal and transcendent." Wordsworth's hanging here "on the perilous ridge" can be seen as emblematically analogous to the grasping by the boy of the Fenwick note on the "Immortality Ode" to a wall or tree to preserve himself from the abyss of idealism. The task of imagination is to preserve the phenomenal world from the destructive thrust of visionary consciousness.

CHAPTER 5: THE SYNTHESES OF IMAGINATION

1 *The Complete Writings of William Blake*, ed. Geoffrey Keynes (London, 1966), p. 782.
2 *Ibid.*, p. 783.
3 *The Prelude*, I ,108–109.
4 *Literary Criticism*, p. 191.
5 Alfred North Whitehead, *Science and the Modern World* (New York, 1948), p. 80.
6 *The Letters of William and Dorothy Wordsworth, The Later Years (1821–50)*, ed. Ernest de Selincourt (Oxford, 1939), I, 134–135.
7 *The Prelude* (1805), VIII, 763.
8 I here assume an identity between the "place of any one thing" and the spatial limits of that thing. Its spatial limits, in other words,

define its place. For the sake of clarity I concentrate in this section upon the question of the nature of the "location" in Wordsworthian space. But my remarks, *mutatis mutandis,* can be applied to the spatial limits of phenomena within that space.

⁹ *Poetical Works,* V, 332, *The Recluse,* I, 571–579.

¹⁰ *The Prose Works of William Wordsworth,* ed. Alexander B. Grosart (London, 1876), III, 464.

¹¹ *The Excursion,* IX, 3–5, 13–16.

¹² Geoffrey Hartman, *Wordsworth's Poetry, 1787–1814* (New Haven, 1964), pp. 84–87, 120–123, *passim.*

¹³ *The Prelude,* I, 466.

¹⁴ *The Excursion,* III, 437–439, 452–461, 462.

¹⁵ *Ibid.,* IV, 755–762.

¹⁶ The poet's task, Wordsworth writes in a letter to John Wilson, is "to rectify men's feelings, to give them new compositions of feeling, to render their feelings more sane, pure, and permanent, in short, more consonant to nature, that is, to eternal nature, and the great moving spirit of things" (*Literary Criticism,* p. 7). The poet thus helps men to sustain hope.

¹⁷ *The Excursion,* I, 78–79.

¹⁸ *The Prelude* (1805), VIII, 760–766. Significantly, the emotional quality of this same entry into London is characterized in an elaborate simile describing an entry into a mysterious cavern; see ll. 711–751. Again, as so often in Wordsworth, the act of apperception is described in terms suggesting an encounter with an abyss or open-ended space.

¹⁹ Henri Bergson, *Time and Free Will,* trans. R. L. Pogson (London, 1910), p. 128.

²⁰ *The Excursion,* III, 400.

²¹ Poulet, *Studies in Human Time,* trans. Elliott Coleman (New York, 1959), p. 29.

²² *The Prelude,* VI, 606. See also n. 20 of chap. 2.

²³ *Literary Criticism,* pp. 34–35.

²⁴ *Poetical Works,* III, 77, ll. 7–8.

²⁵ *Literary Criticism,* p. 129. See also sect. IV of chap. 1 for a consideration of some of the implications of Wordsworth's incarnational theory of language.

²⁶ *The Prelude,* II, 307, 311–322.

²⁷ I here echo Madame de Stael ("It is to re-feel, not recall") who is cited by Poulet in his discussion of romantic affective memory, *Studies in Human Time,* p. 28.

²⁸ *The Prelude,* IV, 256–272.

²⁹ *Ibid.* (1805), XI, 272–273.

³⁰ *Biographia,* I, 202.

³¹ *The Prelude* (1805), XI, 260.

³² *Ibid.* (1850), I, 378, 380, 381, 383, 391–400.

³³ *Ibid.,* ll. 401–404.

³⁴ *Ibid.,* l. 414.

³⁵ *Literary Criticism,* p. 17.

³⁶ *The Prelude* (1805), XI, 334–343.

³⁷ The paradox might be explained in this way: the purpose of

affective memory is, as we have seen, to refeel, not to recollect the past; to recover the "how" of what was felt, not the "what" of what was felt. But the only way to move toward the "how" is through the "what." To recover a mode of past subjectivity requires, therefore, a constitution of the past self as an *object* of remembering consciousness. Thus the very search through the past for a sense of subject *qua* subject stands in paradoxical opposition to the means of this search. That Wordsworth felt he could, and indeed did, overcome this paradox is indicated by his testimony to the "vivifying Virtue" of the "spots of time."

38 Italics mine. The quotation, of course, is from the last two lines of the "Immortality Ode," *Poetical Works*, IV, 285.

39 See n. 48 of chap. 3 for a discussion of the relationship between the sense of immortality experienced by sublime self-consciousness and the sense of immortality experienced, according to Cassirer, by mythical consciousness.

40 "Immortality Ode," ll. 155–156; *Poetical Works*, IV, 284.

41 "English Romanticism: The Spirit of the Age," *Romanticism Reconsidered*, ed. Northrop Frye (New York, 1963), p. 64.

42 *Literary Criticism*, p. 199. One such poorly prepared reader seems to have been Anna Seward, who characterized Wordsworth's poetry as the "egotistic manufacture of metaphysical importance upon trivial themes." Cited by Samuel H. Monk in his "Anna Seward and the Romantic Poets: A Study in Taste," *Wordsworth and Coleridge*, ed. Earl Leslie Griggs (New York, 1962), p. 132.

43 *Literary Criticism*, pp. 13–14. The notion of the poet's mission to extend the kingdom of the sublime is implicit in Wordsworth's description of genius: "Genius is the introduction of a new element into the intellectual universe: or, if that be not allowed, it is the application of powers to objects on which they had not before been exercised, or the employment of them in such a manner as to produce effects hitherto unknown. What is all this but an advance, or a conquest, made by the soul of the poet" (*ibid.*, p. 198)?

44 *Poetical Works*, II, 512.

45 *Ibid.*, II, 331.

46 *Ibid.*, V, 4, ll. 47–55. For a discussion of the "terrestrial paradise" in Wordsworth see Hartman's *The Unmediated Vision* (New Haven, 1954), pp. 26–35.

47 *Poetical Works*, V, 5, ll. 58–59.

48 *Literary Criticism*, p. 11.

49 *Ibid.*, p. 13.

50 *The Prelude*, XIII, 283–287.

51 *Ibid.* (1805), XII, 310–312.

52 *Ibid.*, ll. 51–52.

53 Saint Bernard, *The Steps of Humility*, trans. George Bosworth Burch (Notre Dame, 1963), p. 123.

54 *The Prelude*, XIII, 266–267.

55 *Ibid.*, ll. 227–231, 269.

56 *Ibid.*, ll. 271–275.

57 *Ibid.*, XIV, 209–218.

58 *Ibid.* (1805), XIII, 98–105.

Index

Danby, John F., 142 n. 26
Davie, Donald, on Wordsworth's syntax, 141 n. 11
Dennis, John, on greatness of soul, 151 n. 27
De Quincey, Thomas, on mystery of space, 145 n. 17
Descartes, René, metaphysical assumptions of, and the sublime, 50–54 *passim*
Donne, John, 20, 21, 147 n. 24

Empson, William: on "sense" in Wordsworth, 9; on Wordsworth's vagueness, 140 n. 7

Ferry, David, on Wordsworth's perplexity, 143 n. 2
Frye, Northrop, on metaphorical structure of Romantic poetry, 24–25, 39

Gerard, Alexander (*An Essay on Taste*), 48, 50, 51, 53, 59
Gilson, Etienne, 87

Hartman, Geoffrey, 14, 29, 113; on "apocalypse" in Wordsworth, 54
Herder, Johann Gottfried von, 73
Hopkins, Gerard Manley, and divine immanence, 3, 12, 139–140 n. 5
Hume, David: and the sublime, 50, 59, 61; on thinking as perception, 149–150 n. 11

Ignatius of Loyola, Saint, 20
Intentionality, defined, 5

Kant, Immanuel, 10
Knight, G. Wilson, 143–144 n. 6

Langbaum, Robert, on Romantic "illumination," 145 n. 19
Locke, John: and Wordsworth, 26–27, 28; and Baillie, 57; epistemology of, and apperception, 150 n. 11; and

Coleridge on the symbol, 154–155 n. 11
Longinus, 57, 153 n. 49

Martz, Louis, 20, 31
Milton, John: and Wordsworth, 26, 69; Coleridge on, 80–81
Monk, Samuel, H., 10

Newton, Sir Isaac, and the sublime, 50, 53, 56, 73, 77, 150 n. 16

Ong (S.J.), Walter J., 149 n. 11
Otto, Rudolf, 25; on the "Holy" and the sublime, 143 n. 5

Paul, Saint, 46, 67
Poem, as expression of act of consciousness, 9–10, 12–19, 80–81
Pope, Alexander, 14
Poulet, Georges, 118
Priestley, Joseph (*A Course of Lectures on Oratory and Criticism*), 48, 49, 50, 59–60

Seward, Anna, on Wordsworth, 159 n. 42
Shaftesbury, Earl of, Anthony Ashley Cooper ("The Moralists"), 56
Shelley, Percy Bysshe, 108
Southey, Robert, 131
Spenser, Edmund, 69
Spinoza, Baruch, 2
Sublime, the: as category of experience, 10–11; phenomenology of, 49–60, 72–94; English theorists on, 49–60; Coleridge on, 72–94

Taylor, Jeremy, on hope, 146 n. 20
Thorpe, Clarence DeWitt, 73, 85, 154 n. 1; mentioned, 86, 88
Tuveson, Ernest Lee, on English theorists of the sublime, 49, 56

162

Wasserman, Earl R., on Wordsworth's epistemology, vii

Whitehead, Alfred North (*Science and the Modern World*), on Wordsworth's nature, 109, 112

Wordsworth, Dorothy, 21

Wordsworth, William: on language of his poetry, ix, 132; and natural mysticism, 1–2, 30; and pantheism, 2–3, 45; and use of metaphors of dwelling, 2, 7, 29–30, 45, 69, 134; empiricism of, 4, 5, 98–99; and *anima mundi*, 4, 6; on imagination, 8, 27–28, 67–71, 109, 112, 131; and paradox of *humilitas-sublimitas*, 11–12, 129–137; on relationship between thought and language, 13–14; and organicism, 14, 62; on reading his poetry, 15–16; interior landscape of, 25–30; and marriage of mind and nature, 28–29, 52–53, 64–65, 71, 98–99; and memory, 32–34, 63–65, 119–127; and the "Holy," 25, 40, 143 n. 5; and nature's mythic function, 46; on development of poet's mind, 60–67; and intuition of immortality, 61, 65–67; and the Bible, 65–67, 69; on ancient literature, 69; on Milton, 69; on Spenser, 69; contrasted with Blake, 106–108; and problem of hope, 114–119, 127–128, 145–147 n. 20; poetic program of, 128–136, 158 n. 16; on myth of preexistence, 140 n. 9; on genius, 159 n. 43. Works by: "Essay Supplementary to Preface (1815),", 98, 130; *The Excursion*, viii, 62–67, 71, 113, 114–117, 134; "Immortality Ode," 4, 44, 55, 98; *Lyrical Ballads*, viii, 36; "Preface to *Lyrical Ballads*, 99, 119, 127, 132; "Preface to Poems (1815)," 8, 68–69; *The Prelude*, 14, 27–28, 29, 39, 43, 47, 60–61, 95–98, 101–105, 117, 119, 121–128, 132–137, 151–152 n. 37, 157 n. 41; "Prospectus" to *The Excursion*, viii, 25–26, 28, 39–40, 131–132; *The Recluse* ("Home at Grasmere"), 110–112; "Resolution and Independence," 134, 148–149 n. 3; "The Ruined Cottage," 12; "The Solitary Reaper," 13, 119, 150 n. 11; "The Thorn," 131; "Tintern Abbey," 1–10, 20–46, 145–147 n. 20, and mentioned, 47, 48, 53, 65, 71, 95, 98, 99, 107, 113, 123, 126, 137; "Upon Epitaphs (3)," 13; "With Ships the Sea Was Sprinkled Far and Nigh," 15–19

Young, Edward (*Night Thoughts*), 58